Praying *for* Clean

*A Memoir of Sisterhood,
Substance Abuse, and Second Chances*

TRICIA JACOBSON

Published by Ingenium Books Publishing Inc.
Toronto, Ontario, Canada M6P 1Z2
https://ingeniumbooks.com

International Standard Book Numbers (ISBNs):
Paperback: 978-1-990688-52-2
Ebook: 978-1-990688-53-9

Cover Design by Jessica Bell Design via Ingenium Books
Interior design by Amie McCracken

Praise

"*Praying for Clean* offers readers a deeply personal account of loving someone through addiction. This book is an honest and compassionate testimony of a painful and difficult road toward healing. Tricia Jacobson shares her experience of witnessing her sister's journey through relapse, the hope of recovery, and the power of family love. This story reminds us that behind every statistic is a human being whose life is worth fighting for and that no one is beyond the reach of God's redemption. Anyone who has struggled to understand a loved one caught up in the cycle of addiction will find hope and courage in this book."

PHIL HOPPER, *LIVING YOUR LOVE STORY: TIMELESS WISDOM FOR DATING, MARRIAGE, AND INTIMACY*

"Tricia Jacobson takes us deep into the life of someone who suffers from addiction, her sister. She also reveals the impact the addiction had on herself and her family. When the author worked on finding herself, she was able to reach out and find her sister. The two see the book as a way to create understanding about addictions by removing shame and judgment. It is with that understanding that real change can happen within the broken system of addiction treatment. Eye-opening and inspiring!"

YVONNE CAPUTO, *FLYING WITH DAD: A DAUGHTER. A FATHER. AND THE HIDDEN GIFTS IN HIS STORIES FROM WWII*

"The chaos introduced by family members in the grip of addiction to drugs and alcohol affects so many of us, but we are often silenced by shame. Tricia Jacobson's willingness to openly share stories of struggle, success, and unconditional love in *Praying for Clean* offers the reader hope and solidarity instead. A courageous story of brokenness and redemption."

TANYA HACKNEY, *LEAVING THE SAFE HARBOR: THE RISKS AND REWARDS OF RAISING A FAMILY ON A BOAT*

Contents

Note to Reader

After high school in the late 1990s, my sister Pam managed to survive on the street—sometimes staying a little while with family, then relapsing and returning to a high-risk lifestyle. One time she confessed to me that she felt as though she'd already died a thousand times.

In 2011, Pam found a reason to try to recover. She also gave our family the opportunity to heal our feelings around her addiction. She gave birth to a beautiful child whose remarkable imprint on this earth has changed our world.

Pam is now in her forties. For a good while, she has been living in various secure assisted-living residences. She has received diagnoses of drug-induced dementia, bipolar disorder, and numerous physical ailments. On several occasions, even with the recovery assistance provided by secure facilities and surroundings, she's accessed illegal drugs again. When she is directly under the influence, communication with her can be difficult; when she is in a period of withdrawal, it is impossible.

Pam's lifestyle has taken a toll on her physical body and mental health. She struggles often with understanding what her purpose is in this life. I believe God convicted me to partner with Pam to write our story, not only to make a difference in the lives of others who struggle to understand and come to terms with issues related to addiction and mental health challenges within their families, but to also give Pam another sense of purpose.

Because Pam often has difficulty expressing her thoughts and finding the right words—often also repeating sentences—she's agreed I will take over the writing as a reliable witness. Though she is consulted for content, the narrative can only be based on my perspective because it is the only reliable one I have. Mine is the lens of the younger sister who watched her older sister disappear in that metaphorical scene of seduction and attraction.

The world of addiction is a world where many people step over and walk by the unhoused, then shake their heads and wonder how someone could get that way. It is a world where, when it happens within our own family, we can become fearful and overwhelmed to the point of detaching and trying to forget. It is a world where we are aware but stay silent, keeping the family secrets as long as we are able. It is a world crying out for advocates to validate the humanity of its victims.

Some people think that everyone who is addicted to drugs became that way because they do not have supportive family. Others believe that all who succumb to the kind of life Pam lived, did so due to horrible childhoods. Many deal with their loved one's addiction by keeping it private—or trying to—from the rest of the goings-on in life. Addiction, however, can happen to anyone. It is not selective; it's an all-encompassing power that knocks on everyone's door. It does not discriminate; it can enter the house of anyone who invites it in, willingly or unwillingly.

I'm here to say there is great relief and freedom in opening up and talking about our experiences with loved ones caught in the clutches of addiction. Not only is it cathartic; it might be the way communities can achieve appropriate care for our loved ones. This is the only way to provide them the dignity they deserve.

Prologue:
The Entity

A gentle spring evening settles over our grandparents' home, warm and welcoming. The wide open windows invite the breeze; soft curtains sway in a rhythmic dance to the song of family. Loving energy permeates the little house.

Laughter erupts from a crush of cousins crammed into the living room as they page through the high school yearbooks of our parents. In the dining room, Grandpa leads a game of pitch. Chatter in the kitchen swirls as Aunt Kay mixes a batch of frozen peach daiquiris for Mom and my aunts.

Suddenly, a sharp wind rattles a window and ushers in an entity, dark and intense. It is an accelerant looking to spark a fire where none has existed. It rampages from person to person, seeking a host. It turns toward my sister Pam and shapeshifts into a soft and gentle panda-like stuffy. When she strokes its giant paws, it becomes a whirling temptation, an elixir of promise hiding a toxic layer that melts into her brain, like chocolate left out in the sun, then hardening its venomous sweetness around all the thinking parts.

It slithers back out the window while we hide our eyes from it. The curtains hang lifeless, the house now silent. I count each person. Pam is not there. She has disappeared.

Family members disagree: Was she snatched, was she hypnotized, or did she go willingly, chasing the entity away to protect us? Did we imagine it?

When we finally find Pam sitting on the front porch, we are relieved. We pretend everything will be okay, that she will forget the elixir of toxic sweetness in the experience. But nothing is okay.

It starts one day like a thief in the night and then turns into a constant visitor at our family table. Over time, it takes over. Gone is the song of our family's peace. Something horrible came in and swept away the security and life we knew.

Our gatherings subsequently become less boisterous, laughter is subdued, and once seemingly harmless gossip and teasing now sting. Conversation often begins with welfare-centered questions that revolve around a kind of whodunnit. Questions morph into whys. Everyone now tries to solve the case of the changed sister. Over time, Mom learns she cannot stomach mysteries. Dad increasingly blames himself—he is a Midwestern man, and supposed to be the family protector. My brother will venture elsewhere. And I, the youngest of the three of us, will keep trying to make everything okay as my older sister begins to continuously disappear into dark places.

Part One:
Before the Storm

Chapter 1:
The Dog Park

Most evenings, when the weather is nice, I take my two dogs, Cali and Saint, to the dog park. There are many regulars; I even make it a point to coordinate my schedule with others so our dogs can play together.

It is a perfect August evening, and I head there to enjoy the sunset while the dogs run off some energy. When I arrive, the only other person at the park is a gentleman with whom I've exchanged pleasantries a few times.

Usually, he's there with his wife. However, tonight he sits on the solitary green bench near the middle of the huge park. He's watching his mixed breed when my large Rottweiler puppy, Saint, begins running toward it. Although I know Saint is a gentle giant, I want to reassure the gentleman that everything is okay. My dog will not eat his.

Once I've done that, we chat about the beautiful weather and spectacular sunset. "You're usually here with an adolescent girl," he says.

"That's right. My daughter, Allie, often comes with me," I reply.

"She looks a lot like you, but I have wondered, if you don't mind my asking, if she is adopted?" he asks hesitantly.

"An interesting question," I respond. "We do have similar features, but obvious differences too. The short answer is, yes, she's adopted. The longer story is that my older sister, Pam, battles addiction and mental health issues; she has for nearly twenty-five years. Just over thirteen years ago, she became pregnant. When she was five months along, she asked me if I would adopt her baby when it was born."

"And you did. You agreed right there and then?"

"I sure did," I say proudly.

His bowed head and silence tell me that what I've said means something to him. I break the ice. "Allie's birth brought a kind of restoration to our family. We'd become overwhelmed by Pam's needs. Allie has been a blessing."

We sit in silence a few moments more. Every part of me knows he needs this conversation, because I've sat with others who are carrying so much pain. "I feel like nearly every family I know has someone close to them who battles addiction or mental health struggles," I say.

"I can relate," he says.

"I'm sorry to hear that." All my senses tell me to stay and share the moment. To give him time and hold space. The dogs bounce around us. I ruffle their heads, and they start chasing each other again.

"Can you tell me more about your situation with your sister?" His trepidation makes his inquiry come across a bit formal.

I try to relax the mood; I want to open the door wider for him. "Picture an athletic teen: a girl, but with the muscular build of a football player, the strong arms of a baseball or softball captain, and the bold presence of a strong basketball player. My sister even played a little pro-football!" He leans back into the bench, so I continue.

"She was built for sports, and she was a straight-A student. Multiple college athletic scholarships were offered to her. Add that on top of a gentle soul who often wore her heart on her sleeve. All that was my sister, Pam. We were extremely close growing up. I was convinced she was going to play college sports and pursue her dream of becoming a surgeon, but—"

I break again, ask myself if this is too much for him. He is nodding, so I continue. "But her life took a turn right before her senior year. Her mood shifted, she lost her love for school and sports, and her entire friend group changed. At first, it was hard to understand the changes, but our family discovered she had started using various illegal drugs. What started with weed turned to much harder ones." I give him time to absorb, and catch my own breath, call the dogs, and ground us in an open space.

"From that year on, our lives were never the same. I watched Pam slip away from me. The addiction that followed was tragic. Everything she cared for before addiction became foreign to her. Watching Pam transform into someone unrecognizable was devastating. Then, twelve years into her battle with addiction, she became pregnant." I take a breath mostly to see if he wants me to go on. The dogs circle back and take off again. He leans forward, interested in more. "The thing is, the moment I found out, I knew God wanted me to adopt Pam's precious baby, Allie. Now, the world has the most wonderful girl who has deeply blessed our lives. You know, if you don't mind my sharing my faith, I believe God used the birth of Allie to restore my relationship with Pam."

Something shifts within his already attentive eyes. "I am so sorry to hear about your sister. How wonderful of you to adopt Allie." He looks to the sunset, then back to me. "I have an older daughter who has been going through some rough times—and still is. She is raising a son. It isn't easy for any of us. Her situation causes a lot of stress. She has been in and out of rehab and has struggled with her mental health for quite some time. Her behavior is unpredictable." He still sounds stiff—my heart tells me he's not opened up like this before.

I lean in just a little. "I'm sorry for your situation, too," I say.

"Her name is Caroline," he says, his voice caressing her name.

"That's a beautiful name," I reply.

"After her grandmother," he says. He stretches his legs, his shoulders a little less stiff. "Caroline, like your sister, struggled. In her first year of college, things were tough. I wondered if it was too much pressure on her. She was away from home. She started hanging out with a different friend group—of course she made new friends. 'Dad, I'm just being free,' she'd said when she phoned one holiday to say she wasn't coming home." He breaks for another sunset gaze, very similar to how Pam uses her window to look out and pause the conversation when I visit her.

"Then I accidentally opened a letter from the college," he says. "My wife and I discovered she'd dropped out. When we located her, she was pregnant. We got her to move closer to us. She's raising the child. Her child. His name is Jamie." His eyes grow misty.

"Caroline struggles with parenting. My wife and I worry about our grandson. We don't want him to be taken away from her. We help when there's a crisis, and we see him often. It's just—sometimes she can't care for herself, let alone for Jamie."

"I hear you," I say.

Hope softens his pained expression. "She's working hard to overcome it all. Right now, she's doing better than at the beginning of the year. Jamie isn't missing school as much as he did last year. They both have more contact with us." He looks directly at me for the first time. "It's just so darned hard. Unpredictable. We never know when—"

I nod.

"What I'm trying to say is we don't even recognize her sometimes. She's not the girl we raised. I mean, we love her, but she's so different."

"I understand. I really do. I've learned that when someone we love is battling addiction, they're not the person we remember. We want them back so badly, but they disappear, and we are left to deal with the addiction. It's helpful to remember that it is really the addiction that you're dealing with. It makes it easier to set boundaries and practice some tough love," I say.

"Aha," he replies, "because they're not who they were. It's like they *are* the addiction. That viewpoint might make it easier on my wife and I when we, for example, speak to her social worker." He closes his eyes. "Wow, I can't believe I just told you all that. My wife and I don't often talk about it with others, but I felt comfortable telling you."

He opens his eyes, and it is as though years of bottled-up stress have lifted from his shoulders.

"I mean it. I really can't believe I shared all of that with you." His shoulders soften even more.

"Thank you for doing so. It's brave to share. Healing too. There are more people than we realize who can relate to our stories, but they're uncomfortable telling their own because of fear of judgment or a lack of understanding. That was me for years. After Allie was born, I realized I needed to be more of an advocate for Pam, which ultimately meant I needed to write and tell her story—our story—because we all feel less alone when we know others can relate in some small way. It's a sharing of a burden," I say.

"You're a safe place to talk about it. Thank you for being a listening ear and being someone who made the time." His dog has returned. He ruffles the mutt's head.

"I'm glad I could. The struggles can be truly inconceivable unless someone's been there. Please know, you're not alone."

He looks up and smiles. "I know that now," he says.

His saying "I know that now" brings tears to my eyes. My sharing has helped. What if I could share with everyone? My mind races. I slow it down. That's what I've been trying to do. It is validation.

"Tricia," I say my own name. I realize I don't say it a lot.

"Robert." He offers his hand.

I bring myself back into his smile, the two of us on the bench, the dogs gathering round us for attention. This conversation will have a lasting impact on both of us, I think.

I am still thinking about Robert when I get home. How devastating for him and his wife, not knowing where their daughter was after that letter from college arrived.

I wish I had told him more, like all the ways that Pam's addictions have affected me. And how it's okay to feel frustrated—angry even.

Even as someone free of addictions, I've seen the worst of myself in my disappointment with Pam—or I should say: with Pam's addiction—annoyed by her choices and their intrusion into my life and on how I make my way through the world.

Anger and resentfulness have often crept in despite my best efforts. In the past, and occasionally now, my anger hadn't stopped with Pam; I've raged about drug lords and cartels, cursed the government, and tied myself up in knots over them or systematically blamed a group of people I couldn't even identify. None of that was productive, but it was how I coped. Talking about addiction would take me in circles, always leaving me exhausted and exasperated.

Finally, I learned to start each day reminding myself that I loved a person, not a behavior. That helped a lot. But, sometimes, as the day progressed, if I got a phone call from authorities, or if my sister called to ask for money for a pair of jeans or a laptop—which I knew she would sell, but I didn't want to believe it—each time, the impatience and annoyance crept in. I'd become irritable, then apologize for my irritability, then wonder why it was me who had to apologize. I'd send curses in every direction in my frequent "I didn't sign up for this" rants to God. I'd go to bed wondering which of us was in the relentless cycle: Pam or me?

I'd toss and turn, get up at three in the morning, go to the window, wonder where she was sleeping. I'd get frustrated that I wasn't in my own bed—all because of them. I wrestled with guilt—what could I have done so that all of this never happened? I'd break down and cry until I was a puddle on the floor over my own perceived failings. Then I'd collect myself, rushing around the house to find some basket of hope. I'd ask myself: *Where did I last see that basket? What was in it?* Eventually, I'd remember: I was not alone. There were many people with addicted loved ones. I developed the mantra that hope is to faith as mindset is to re-framing. I had to reframe the story so I could understand it and release it.

Chapter 2:
Cow Surgery

I was face down in the grass on a warm summer's day in 1987. The sun beat down on me as I counted to twenty. A pair of short overalls draped over my tall-for-a-five-year-old slender frame. Pam, at seven, had cut the legs for me to make them wearable in hot weather. No shirt underneath. As always, I was barefoot— shoes were only required for going into town.

"Nineteen … twenty!" I ran toward the barn on our fifteen-acre farm. I was sure Pam and our brother, Heath, were hiding there. My unbrushed hair blew in the wind as I ran to find them in our daily game of hide-and-seek. Our cow, Agnes, was drinking water from the trough. I stroked her head a few times, slapped a big kiss on the soft patch by her nose, then jumped the fence in front of the barn. I began sifting my way through the stacked hay bales, but there wasn't so much as a peep. I ran back toward the house, and a faint sister-giggle came from the storm shelter Dad had built between the house and garage. Young as I was, I understood the need for it: tornados. Even though our house was an earth-contact home, with extensive connection to the ground around it, the shelter was essential in Missouri. We were in a state which forms part of the huge area known as the Tornado Belt.

"I found you!" I shouted.

When Heath and Pam traipsed out of their spot, I told them it was my turn to hide, but Heath announced it was time to catch crawdads. "I'll grab the bucket and meet you two by the pond," he said. The days were long and magical, and we made them into what we wanted them to be.

ॐ

I pause the reel from summer '87 and open my eyes and ears only for a few moments of July 2024; the flight attendant asks if I'd like a beverage. I consider asking for root beer, knowing full well they won't have it. I order soda water and pretend it's my favorite licoricey drink.

One sip tumbles me back to the '80s.

ॐ

Dad, the hardest-working man I've ever known, a carman at the Union Pacific Railroad. Mom, a stunning Maltese-American, a home-health nurse who never knew a stranger. They had three children. Heath, the eldest with seven years on me, was the ringleader of our great childhood adventures. Pam, the middle child, was my everything, the cat's meow, the bee's knees: my best friend.

We moved to the country when I was five, and my life only seemed to come alive in a storybook way when Dad built the house on fifteen acres in the country of Pleasant Hill, just southeast of Kansas City. The farm was surrounded by acres and acres that became a playground for endless thrills. Christopher Robin and Winnie-the-Pooh had their Hundred Acre Wood; Heath, Pam, and Tricia had ours.

Pam and I were inseparable, connected by an unbreakable bond. Devoted to each other, we were fearless. Entire children's books could have been written about our adventures.

We'd run out of the house, barefoot, as the sun appeared on the horizon, and we wouldn't return home until almost dark, just in time for dinner—without a swing or metal slide in sight. Barefoot down the gravel road, over the bridge Dad made for us, and past what we thought of as our pet owl, Owlie, always perched in an oak next to the bridge. That road was as magical to us as the wardrobe was to Lucy and her brothers in *The Chronicles of Narnia*. It led to endless possibilities: mud baths in the ditch after a good rain, buckets of crawdads, riding bareback and harnessless on the neighbor's horses, and fishing excursions. We had gainful employment too: getting paid with candy for collecting eggs for a neighbor whose house reeked with an unforgettable scent—one part old man who rarely bathed, and another part from his hens, which he sometimes allowed to roam freely through his home.

Even bedtime was an event, a concert of crickets heard through the open window in our safe and quiet corner of the country. This little slice of heaven filled me so full of wonder and love, I grew up knowing that the world can be beautiful and good, and that nature can be healing.

⊰⊱

"Are you going to finish your drink?" asks the flight attendant.

"I'm sorry. I'll drink it quickly."

"You don't have to be sorry," she says. "I'm just here to see if you want something else."

The flight attendant is right. I don't have to be sorry. I've gotten caught in a gap between nostalgia and the present; been going there a lot.

I think about that word, *sorry*—so many meanings: apologetic, sorrowful, repentant. I've used it a lot. Heard it even more. Especially from Pam. Having lived in a cycle of need and shame for so long, it became habitual for her to apologize for the cycles of disruption and dysregulation. Which are of course nicer words for *all hell breaking loose.* I'd become so sick of that word—until I realized it was also an invitation to understand forgiveness.

"One more story," I say.

"I beg your pardon?" says the flight attendant.

"I mean, no, not finished. I mean, yes, I'm thirsty. I mean, I'm good with it."

And I am thirsty. Thirsty for the past. I'm coming out of weeks of extra work advocating for people with mental illness and drug addiction, and discussions with Pam's public guardian. I've been juggling business with the joys of my life, all the girls I've come to love and mother over the years: Kailey, Grace, Reagan, Allie.

Oh, how I wish I could tear a thousand calendar pages back to Pam and me on the farm. But then there would be no Allie. There might not even be a Grace, Kailey, or Reagan in my life. Even if wishes could come true, I would not want a world without my girls. Why couldn't things be simple, like they were when I was five, six, seven, eight? And how many years had I been dealing with this? Twenty, twenty-five?

I am still in the air. In my head, I'm wearing those same cut-off overalls.

⁂

I was about six and Pam was eight. We chattered away as we headed to one of our special hidden places: a small, dirty pond, invisible to a passerby because of the overgrowth of trees. Our brother and a handful of neighbor kids trailed along the path too. We loved this place like we loved all the places we explored.

It didn't faze us when we ducked under the last vine and saw a dead, bloated cow floating in the middle of the pond.

Pam knew everything and told me that rigor mortis had set in—and that if the cow was poked, it might explode. "But I'm not going to poke it," she said. "I'm going to perform my first ever brain surgery."

She was convinced the operation would look great on her future resume and, of course, lead her to a renowned career at the greatest hospital in the land. First, however, we had to secure the patient.

We couldn't quite reach the dead cow, though we made endless attempts to pull it in with long broken tree branches that had fallen to the ground in the windstorm of the night before. Plan B was required; fortunately, Pam was filled with the alphabet. She did what any ambitious future brain surgeon would do: She jumped into the pond.

I may have been a little kid, but I knew the pond wasn't clean and a person could get sick from the germs in the water's stagnant depths. Pam was unwavering in her attempts to retrieve the cow, and her attempts proved fruitful as she gripped the cow's ear and breaststroked with her other arm.

When she waded to shore, we realized the cow was so heavy we wouldn't be able to get her onto land. Even with more of us—and there were more, but they didn't want to join in—we could never pull her out. It didn't matter to Pam. Her face combined a satisfied grin with a scientific calculation, victorious at securing her first patient: Betsy.

As Betsy floated bloated and deep in decay, Pam insisted I watch over the patient. "Make sure she doesn't float back," said Pam. She ran in the direction of the house to fetch the tools required for surgery. I stood at the ready, my tiny hands tingling in anticipation of grabbing Betsy's head should an errant current begin to lap and call her back to the center of the cesspool.

I stood proud, watching over the smelly cow for quite a while. Heath and the neighbor kids were too impatient to wait for Pam's return, and I was left without an audience. My responsibilities were too great to abandon. Pam was my best friend. I'd never leave her to do a messy job like this on her own. *She'll be back.* I stood like a soldier on watch duty.

I was glad the others were gone because now, Pam and I could be the dynamic duo. Deep into imagining how well I was guarding the scene, Pam's delightful screams arrived before she did. She came into view, her surgeon's tools and paraphernalia raised high. My excitement exploded as I told her that while she was gone, I'd defeated giants, fought off aliens, and obliterated the poop monster—all in the name of defending Betsy and saving Pam's medical career. She high-fived me for my victories and then commanded me to wash my hands in preparation for the operation. The only water available to us was that of the dirty pond, but in her mind, it was probably a stainless-steel basin filled with antibacterial cleanser and fresh, clean water.

She carefully placed a surgical gown on me: Mom's red-and-white plaid cooking apron. On my hands, a pair of surgeon's assistant gloves exactly like Dad's yellow, grease-covered, leather work gloves. She asked me to glove her with Mom's pink rubber dishwashing gloves. We finished by dressing the surgeon in Dad's blue-and-black plaid button-up shirt that usually rested on the coat hook near the front door.

I completed my duties with pride; there was no way to wipe the big smile off my face. Pam's surgical attempts were, in reality, disgusting and unsuccessful. There had been no cracking the skull or peering into the cavities of the brain, but Pam celebrated anyway. In this story, the only element of fiction was that we imagined, using the precise movements of her surgical hands, Pam was able to bring Betsy back to life.

❧

"Finished?" says the flight attendant.

"Isn't it amazing how fact is stranger than fiction?" I ponder.

She holds open a garbage bag with her gloved hands. "Are you a writer?"

She asks this and at the same time I am wondering whether, in this sister collaboration of a memoir, anyone will believe the cow story.

Chapter 3:
Daydreaming

I'm still on the plane, with the sun streaming through the window. It feels like I'm under the dryer at a salon—warmed from the top down. I close my eyes. I squint and angle my head to see the ground far below. I love imagining and I love summer.

A warm, gentle breeze blows my hair across my sunglasses, and I drink ice water from a fancy goblet while sinking into a comfortable chair on the patio of a contemporary restaurant. People-watching is good on this patio because it's between a busy street and a park. I pull out my lip gloss from my handbag to reapply it before my Pam arrives.

We're meeting for brunch at our favorite spot. She always gets the migas and I ask for the classic Benedict. I've taken the liberty of ordering her a mimosa; she enjoys an occasional drink, and I know she's had a hectic week at the hospital. My glass sweats in the late morning sun. As I wipe it down with my napkin, a soft hand touches my shoulder and, before I can respond, a kiss is planted on the side of my cheek.

"Hi, Toots. Fancy meeting you here," says Pam.

"It's about time you showed up." I clasp her hand. "The way you're always running late, people would think you had some demanding career as a surgeon." We laugh.

"How are your girls?" asks Pam. "I can't wait to see them this weekend.

Warm waves fill my core. "Great. How's Allie?" I ask. "I haven't heard from her since she called to tell me she'd hit two out-of-the-park home runs."

We catch up on our news and the activities of our beautiful children.

Our orders arrive.

"It's hard to believe," I say. "Feels like yesterday we were running around barefoot on the farm."

"It sure does." Pam is staring out beyond the patio to the thicket of trees.

"I have exciting news to share," I say.

"Let me guess. You've finally accepted I'm the better basketball player." Pam delivers her joke with a grin.

"Yeah, that will never happen," I say.

I tell her my eldest found out she's having a girl; I talk about how excited I am to become a grandma.

Pam tells me she's talked to Mom, who is planning a trip to Malta in September. "Let's go with her. Even though it's hard to step away from my schedule, we don't get enough time together," Pam says.

We spend the rest of our time together yammering on about our family in Malta, and sharing gratitude for the lives we've made for ourselves.

If only. If only it could be this way. What I'd give to be able to tell anyone that Pam and I had this exchange at brunch—that we even had brunch. I can only imagine the joy in catching up on the latest or talking about what the kids' futures will be like. Well, that's what I'm doing: imagining.

It's hard to imagine Allie as not my daughter. But if I can squeeze in a daydream of how I wish it were, then I'd be able to imagine that Pam not only carried her and birthed her, but it's also a perfect world because she's parenting her.

I don't know if it's healthy for me to escape into that daydreaming; I don't even want to know.

Pam never became a surgeon. We've never sat on a patio, sipping from goblets that glistened in the sun. Nor did we ever talk about how she made time for a trip to Malta with Mom, nor how there was never an invite for the girls and me to join her and Allie on that trip—because she never got to make that trip. The times that we've sat together, visiting, it's much like when I go and see her at the residential facility meant to keep her safe.

Again, I wonder how fair it is to have secured a public guardian who helps decide where Pam lives. I could never have been a good full-time guardian to her. I had too much on my plate, and I wanted to protect Allie as much as possible from the life-style Pam was living. I am Pam's sister. I also have a life. Pam has now been provided representation that is appropriate for her. The public guardian ensures that there are healthy boundaries between us, and respects Pam's privacy to the extent possible, while inviting me to assist in the decision-making. I can remain her sister instead of her caretaker.

The broken and the grateful within me recognizes the broken and the grateful in you. Each of us can find common ground with one another: We go to the store, go to weddings and funerals, watch movies, wait by the phone for hours. We never know what those calls may bring, but we always anticipate them anyway.

Chapter 4:
Toots and PK

In Pam's perfect world without addiction, my café daydream would be true as well.

Instead, in reality, she has lived between the worlds of the streets, squats, suppliers, and traffickers—and some attempted but failing semblance of a normal family life. We needed to find her a place where she had some routine. She is there now because I lobbied for that public guardian some years ago. I've often wondered where the line is—the one I crossed to keep her safe at the expense of her freedom. It has been a series of decisions made on a tightrope.

Though Pam's lived in other facilities, she's currently in a small residential facility—a nursing home for senior citizens—that, while not perfect for her, provides some supervision to help her deal with the physical, mental, and emotional fallout from her decades of drug use. Pam is only forty-four, and some of the other eleven residents are double her age.

It is summer of 2024, and I visit her in that residence. Yesterday I was on a plane, thinking about her. About what I will ask. Say.

Am I ready to listen?

"Hey, Toots," she says as I enter the room.

"Hey, PK." Toots and PK: our names for each other.

"Take a load off. Someone brought some soda. Root beer. Want some?"

"That's nice. Sure, in a bit. I came to ask you something."

"It's there for the takin'." She shifts in her chair.

Pam's a kinda masculine forty-something, a wide-shouldered gal, and the years have only toughened her expression. Even when her face is in soft-smile mode, it's the football-game cheering variety. She's not as physically active as she was in her teens, but has retained her broad chest and muscular look.

We take up very different kinds of space, even though we share the same parents and childhood. My six-foot, slender build is made for efficiency; it's often wound like a tight spring as I combine frenetic energy and caffeine to allow myself to take on another project, idea, or investment. I waste nothing—neither time nor steps—for either physical or metaphorical kinds of efforts.

"Maybe I'll get that drink." I don't often stall, but this conversation is important. I want to get it right.

She braces herself to push off her chair. It's ironic how she now has to look up to me from her five-foot seven-inch frame, when in childhood, it was always me looking up to her for leadership.

"No, go sit and be comfortable. I've got this." I sense relief as she takes the few steps back to the soft armchair. She winces: a cramp, arthritis, abdominal pain? She's been to a lot of medical appointments in the last few years.

"Hey sis, will you bring me a glass of ..." Pam pauses as she does often when trying to recall certain words.

"Root beer?" I finish her sentence.

"Yes, root beer."

I pull a chair closer to her, so we're face to face. I see myself, our brother, mother, father, children, and grandparents in hers.

"PK, I want to know if you'd be willing to tell me what you remember about the twelve years before Allie was born. There's some I know, but a lot I don't. It's important to include in the book so you can help others through your experiences."

"Isn't the book you want to write about our childhood?"

"Yes, sort of."

"What do you mean sort of?"

"I want the book to tell our full story. The good and the bad. I want to share some of the amazing childhood memories we share. I want to share how things got hard for both of us. I want to shed light on mental health and addiction, and I want to share how God used the birth of Allie to bring restoration to our relationship."

"Willing to talk about what I remember before Allie. Oh, Toots, I've forgotten more than I remember. But wait. First, you have to promise to make sure the book has a part about how I played semi-pro football with Kansas City Glory."

"Absolutely. The football will definitely be included." I need to steer her back on track. "Just as important is to talk about the struggle, though. Remember, this book is about two sisters who had a wonderful relationship—and still do—but how it was sort of torn apart for a while by one of the sisters' battle with addiction, and the other sister not knowing how to navigate that."

"I remember now. It's about us. The bad stuff."

"The good stuff too. Other people might see themselves in our stories and see how we coped. Not in a *how to cope* sort of way but rather a *here's how it was for us, and so here's how it might be for them.*"

"The way we were. The way we are."

"What it was like for you. The good, the bad, the ugly. If you're willing. The purpose is to show people that when their loved ones are in the depths of addiction, they're not alone—even though it might feel that way."

A pause. *What is she thinking?*

"Hey, Toots, I think I'd like some more of that root beer."

"Here, take mine. I haven't started yet. I'll go pour another. And don't think I haven't noticed you're using my nickname—Toots."

"Your nickname—Toots."

As I'm pouring another root beer, I ask, "Are you okay to talk about the book? We can go as specific as you like."

"You decide. Hopefully I remember. We're doing this to help others, right?"

"I think there'll be some value for us too. I was thinking on the plane ride back home from my trip about hope. How I think we've both come to understand that most of us are nothing without hope, and powerless without faith. I used to get angry with this whole situation."

"I'm sorry." Almost a whisper.

"No. It's okay. I mean I didn't know how to handle my own stuff and how much of yours I could take on." I try to sound reassuring. "But a shift toward a deeper understanding took place for me when I took my thoughts out of the box and began to reorganize them. Reframing. It took time. I think it might be like that for others: their own version of going beyond coping so that they can come to terms with their situations and find space for forgiveness, acceptance, and even advocacy."

"Do you want me to start talking about what it was like?"

"No, I'm sorry. Rambling on." I take a sip of my drink. "The point I was making is when we can gather our body, mind, and soul into one internal and intentional meeting, we can rise. It wasn't easy for me. It won't be easy for most. But, as the sibling without the addiction, I had to learn to understand addiction because of our journey."

"Well, your changes for sure helped me. When I was open to help. Which was often too late." Another pause. "Hey, Toots, this isn't the future we dreamed of when we were children."

Pam is already using the window to disconnect from conversation. Or maybe she is thinking. Maybe I am judging and she's just gathering her words. Who am I to say what goes on in her mind? Now it's my turn to look out the window. I didn't and still don't know everything.

But she is right: This isn't the future we'd dreamed of. Nor did her situation turn out to be our ideal life vision of her fulfilling her medical-school dreams, yet her value is still not a fraction less than that of the doctor who saves lives through prevention, treatment, or surgery.

I've told myself a thousand times that I can be frustrated, I can feel anger; that it's okay to get frustrated and irritated because I've had to reschedule work around one of her crises, do a meeting on the phone on the way to help with some calamity or other. I've also reminded myself of the value of boundaries. I work on maintaining a healthy equilibrium—highfalutin' words for *keeping it all real.*

The emotional costs have been high for our family—entire lives disrupted—but Pam returned to hero status in my eyes through a kind of admiration for her resiliency and the energy to hang in there and restart, time after time. I see her battling the effects of addiction with everything she has. Not that I put her on a pedestal. I have started to see us as equals inside our own journeys, both opposed to illicit substances: one of us so severely affected by addiction that she has a public guardian—the legal term for that person is *ad litem*—ensuring her safety; and one of us advocating for shifts in a system within a system that umbrellas addiction under mental health. One that seems to have more dead ends than avenues to solution.

Pam taught me a lot about me: my limits and boundaries; the pieces of myself at the extremes of my creativity; the strength of my values; the management of a list of sneaky, life-stalling emotions, including my own guilt and shame. There has been much to unpack around perceived failed and strained relationships, and not measuring up to unrealistic standards. Mine and others'.

"Hey, Earth to Toots." Her voice draws me back to the here and now. "We were working on the book, right?"

"You know what I was thinking? How you were born with a heart of gold and that huge personality. Your kindness and intelligence shone through from the start—and so did your competitive nature. You had that *go big or go home* attitude. I sense that coming through again right now."

"And you? You were born with those rose-colored glasses on."

"I like to think of it as the soul of a helper; I was created to serve. I evolved into someone who helps others to find a path of understanding, forgiveness, and peace during their experiences with their loved ones. And as I have, I've started to find my own strength in helping myself first."

"Listen to you, all grown up."

"It's a calling, Pam. I want to help others. You're part of that." *Maybe I need to explain this better?* "Just as I discovered some solutions to help you—which helped all of us—I am pushing for solutions for everyone. I am seeking answers at personal, community, and national levels and will continue to do so. My soul of a helper has been morphing into the spirit of an advocate."

"You're not as scared as you used to be." Her insight takes me by surprise.

"I think you're right. I was trapped in that kind of scared where I didn't want to share our story. I did not even want to know the full details of your story. I have arrived at a place where I am no longer ashamed to own our story—or tell it." I turn so that I'm facing her directly. "I think you did too, PK. Someone once said to me, 'You have to turn your mess into your message.'"

"*Mess into message*," she savors the words. "I like that."

"This story of ours," I say, remembering how it began on a fifteen-acre farm south of Kansas City, with the most idyllic childhood a person could ask for, "took some radical and unexpected turns, didn't it?"

Pam turns to me. "You've changed a lot. I've got a ways to go, but I can't go back," she says wistfully. "I burned those bridges."

"But you can go forward," I reassure her. "You *are* going forward. I realized that the other day after we visited. I went home and got the dogs and went to the dog park. And I met someone there."

Her face lights up. "I love dogs! Did you take Allie? Did you meet Allie there?"

"Allie was with friends. I went alone."

"But with the dogs, so not alone."

I steer the conversation back to the man I met at the dog park. "I met someone at the dog park who'd seen me there before with Allie. He asked me about her—if she was mine, biologically—which led to us chatting about our story, which led him to open up to me about his daughter who has had struggles similar to yours." I pause and take another sip of my drink before continuing. "When we were done visiting, he told me he couldn't believe he'd told me all of that because he and his wife rarely talk about it with others."

"At the dog park," Pam repeats with furrowed brows, "you met a stranger."

"I've seen his wife and him there lots of times. Remember what I've always said about mom: She never knew a stranger."

"Which means?"

"That she considered everyone someone worth knowing. We are all connected."

Pam seems to ponder this for a few seconds, then asks, "You said he has a daughter?"

"Yes. Caroline. She has a son, Jamie. She's struggling, PK."

"Why don't they talk about it?"

"Well, our family didn't either, PK," I remind her. "We had an elephant in the room."

"Me." She avoids my gaze.

"The addiction. You weren't you when you were under the influence of drugs."

"Which was a lot."

I let that statement hang in the air for a moment. "Your question was about why people don't talk about it," I continue. "I think people feel alone in their struggles. I could tell it was a relief for him to have someone to talk to about it without judgment or feelings of shame."

"Feelings of shame. Wow, yeah, I know a lot about the feelings of shame."

"Me too." I'm not sure if she believes me. "You know what a good friend once told me? He said that shame is a worthless emotion. I couldn't agree more. I think that shame is from the enemy, so we need to let go of shame and let God use our story to help others."

"Helping others. That means a lot."

Window time for both of us. We drift as each of us find and settle our thoughts.

Pam's next question startles me. "Did Dad ever tell you about the time he came to that really bad drug house in downtown Kansas City and pulled me out of it and took me home?"

"Yeah, it's scary to think about and, honestly, it goes to show how much we all love you. You know how gentle Dad is, and how much he hates confrontation? He still went there." *For you, PK.* "Love knows no bounds."

"If you could have seen that place," she says, seemingly staring through space and time. "It was bad. I don't even know how many people were in that place. No running water. Some of the windows boarded up. A lot of moaning. Just like you see in the movies when people trip over others because they're just scattered about and, well, basically dying. It's like no one cares about them, and they don't know how to care about themselves. The people I was running with were really, really, really, bad. Can't believe they didn't hurt Dad when he came to get me."

God was watching over both of you, I think.

"I should be dead. I really should. I overdosed so many times. You don't know all the times." She stares at the floor, then speaks so softly I can barely hear her. "Did you know Heath—Bub—saved me after I had overdosed?"

I didn't know it had happened at the time. He told me years later.

"I was so stupid," Pam continues. "Even brought a drug dealer to Dad's to try to get Dad to pay him because I couldn't. How stupid was that?" She raises her voice. "How stupid that I'd risk Dad's life like that?"

"It wasn't you. It was the addiction. The drugs." *I have to make her understand.* "Back then, every time we were in the middle of hard stuff, we weren't dealing with Pam; we were dealing with the drugs and addiction."

"Not really me." She ponders this. "Yeah, I can see that. When I was on drugs, I didn't care about who I hurt or what people thought of me. I didn't have the energy to care. My brain only went to one place: the drugs. When I needed more, I'd do anything. Like that time I stole checks from Mrs. Bailey. I knew she had money, so I stole her checks and cashed them so I could buy more drugs. But I ended up in jail for it." She looks at me again. "I used to steal so much, Toots. It's embarrassing to think about it all now. I used to constantly ask or bully people into giving me money so I could get my next high. I did that to you."

She looks into her lap.

"I've tried every drug imaginable," she continues. "I've done them all. Many times, I did not even know what I was really taking. Most of us do not. If you only knew the people I used to hang out with. Some of them were really awful, but I didn't care. All most of us want is to be with people who make you feel normal—and they made me feel normal because they wanted the same things I wanted. But they were bad people. And I was one of them. I stole cars and broke into houses. Sometimes I'd wake up in a place and have no idea how I got there. There were times I opened my eyes and there'd be a needle in my arm. I even remember waking up in the woods."

She lifts her head and meets my eyes.

"It's a life I never could have imagined, you know, when we were little. All I thought about then was sunshine and success. I really wanted to be a brain surgeon, Trish." The sudden switch from her nickname for me doesn't go unnoticed. "I wanted to do a lot of things. I could have been anything if I hadn't become an addict. I could have been as smart as you. I could have had a family also, and a house, and driven cool cars. Hell, I could have been an astronaut. Instead, I pissed my life away. Pissed it away on drugs. Mom and Dad taught us how to work hard and instead, I ruined my life with drugs."

"Listen, I know you beat yourself up for the way things have turned out in your life. And, hey, I know I've said life is about choices. But when we're talking addiction, then we know it's a whole new ball game." I reach for her hand. "Addiction is an enemy that gets a powerful hold on people. Even strong people like you. This is all part of why I wanted to write this book and share your story." *Our story.* "To build awareness."

"There are lots of bad things back there. Maybe I am strong, but it's hard to see the good." My heart breaks again for her. "The book, though, if people can feel—what did you say? Not alone?"

"In sharing as much as you can, you are creating change." I give her hand a squeeze that I hope is reassuring. "You're brave in sharing. In a way, you're letting people into your life. All the readers who will get to know you and then maybe know their loved ones a little more because of you."

"You're gonna tell it all, right?" There's a sudden urgency in her voice. "Tell people it can happen to anyone. It can happen to them even though they think it can't. I don't want them to think I'm nothing, even though lots of times I think I am."

One more crack in the heart. Bring on the gold to fill in the space. Pour it in like the Japanese do through the art of kintsugi. Let me remember the lyrics of Leonard Cohen when he sings about how the cracks are how the light gets in.

"Let's remember them as they were. As we were," Pam suggests.

Chapter 5:
The Big, Loud Maltese Side

Pam and I were born into two large families, many of whom lived in the same community as us or in one nearby. Both sets of grandparents lived within a mile of each other, so we had the joys of growing up with all of them.

Mom's side of the family is the Maltese/Italian version of the Portokalos family from *My Big Fat Greek Wedding*.

Mom was one of six kids. Heath, Pam and I have eleven first cousins on her side. Much like the character Toula mentions in *MBFGW*, our family is loud, and everyone is in one another's lives and business ... all the time. When Pam and I were children, we rarely had a moment alone to think because people were always around eating and talking, and did I mention eating?

All fourteen of us cousins and all our aunts and uncles gathered at my grandparents' every weekend, and often throughout the week—grandchildren running everywhere, wreaking havoc at their house: kickball in their backyard, tormenting our grandparents' elderly neighbors who despised loud kids and cursed about us always jumping their fences to fetch our balls.

While we kids made messes, the moms sat in the kitchen, talking about shopping excursions, coloring one another's hair with box dye, or catching up from the last time they saw one another—even though that might have been the day before. The dads sat around the dining room table with Grandpa Hammons, all of them playing that ever-present game of pitch.

When my grandparents weren't bickering, they'd slow-dance in the kitchen to whatever song Grandma Hammons had playing on the radio, which was attached to the bottom of the cabinet above the coffee pot. Despite our Maltese heritage, we had Taco Saturday every week. I must imagine that somewhere there is a Mexican-American family who enjoys Pasta Saturday. Sundays, after Grandma returned from church, Grandpa prepared pot roast with all the fixings. Later, the family crammed into the living room to watch the week's episode of *Hee Haw*.

Grandma is a devout, Jesus-loving Catholic. She never missed Wednesday Mass. On any given weekday, she'd be cleaning or working on something around the house and talking to herself in Maltese. Grandpa spent his time watching sporting events on television, or reading a book at the kitchen table, coffee cup at the ready.

A bunch of cousins regularly spent the night there. If someone were to walk into our grandparents' home on a Saturday or Sunday morning, they'd be greeted with the sight of kids sleeping on couches, on reclining chairs, on the floor, in the spare bedroom, or even under the dining room table where they'd built a fort. Every Saturday morning, after our morning tradition of crowding around their television to watch the revolutionary MTV, all the cousins and aunts piled into several cars and spent entire days at the shopping mall, Independence Center. It was a weekly tradition for the younger ones, before sports and activities took over. It was a blast to be with the cousins, running around the mall as our mothers shopped, but a full day was too much; we often got stuck there longer than we wanted, because of Grandma's habit of venturing off on her own without telling anyone. In a time without cellphones, we had to create search parties and have a meeting place to keep checking in at. We learned to become as organized as a recon unit in a war—except we were a lot louder about it.

Grandpa always turned his favorite holiday, the Fourth of July, into a massive, elaborate celebration, spending what must have been a month's salary on fireworks. He barbequed chicken thighs on the black Weber as he watched us shoot off rocket after rocket. One time, we shot a bottle rocket into the neighbor's yard and set fire to their trampoline. Instead of getting upset with us kids, Grandpa walked over to the neighbors and told them he'd buy them a new one.

Dozens upon dozens of times we'd all be at our grandparents' house to watch *Shag*, the 1988 movie that came out in the wake of the *Dirty Dancing* craze. Set in 1963, four teenage girlfriends escape their middle-class parents for a few days for an adventure in Myrtle Beach. The film featured dance contests, girlfriend shenanigans, and cute boys; it's a wonder those VHS tapes didn't wear out.

※

"That teenage neighbor babysitting us when our parents were still together and went on dates," Pam says with a laugh. "Forced us to watch *Dirty Dancing* on repeat."

I burst out laughing too. "Talk about getting a little too cultured as young children! We watched it so many times! Remember how we reenacted the 'Come here, lover boy' scene to annoy that sitter?"

"Remember the new television? A twenty-five inch screen!"

"Those after school specials."

"You changed the channels with your toes."

"No! … Wait—yes, I did!" We are both screaming with laughter now.

When she catches her breath, Pam says in a more serious tone, "Baby Jessica."

"Tell me more."

"You were about five or six. Baby Jessica fell down into a well."

"Oh, right. They covered it on television. We sat transfixed watching, what was it, CNN?"

"Look it up on your phone."

I take out my phone, type *Baby Jessica* into the search engine, and scan the first article that comes up. "You're right. Baby Jessica. 1987. She was eighteen months old and fell down the well in her aunt's yard. Fifty-eight hours to get her out, with CNN giving around-the-clock coverage."

"We snuck out of bed in the middle of the night to check for updates. And I remember, clearly, Toots, that Ronald Reagan claimed everyone became godmothers and godfathers to Jessica."

"You remember that? You were only seven or eight."

"Right about that time you were going through a stage where you were afraid of everything. Mom and Dad pulled our bunkbed away from the wall so you could squeeze between the bed and the wall, then I'd pile blankets on top—you'd ask me to—so that no robber or alien could find you."

"I'd forgotten about that."

Pam smiles. "I'm on a roll." Mischief in her voice. "You'd sleep with a vinyl ET that had creepy-feeling skin which started to peel after a few years. How funny that you slept with the very thing you were afraid of. Look that up too." She gestures towards my phone.

"ET came out in 1982."

"The year you were born."

"Sheesh, you're spilling out the joy like it's yesterday."

"Remember when Mom and Dad surprised us with a Nintendo Entertainment System—Christmas in July? It came with *Super Mario Bros.*, *Duck Hunt*, and a light-gun accessory, as well as an extra controller. We had to sit super close to the TV because the Nintendo cords were so short."

"Your specifics are flipping mind-blowing," I say, relieved that her long-term memory seems to still be working.

Then Pam continues. She really is on a roll today. "Somewhere in that cobweb-filled attic of our childhood home is a collection of the McDonald's Happy Meal toys we collected."

"We couldn't have cared less about the cheeseburgers, French fries, cookies and soda. We were there for the toys."

"Those Mr. Potato Heads, Muppets, Garfield stuff ..." Her voice drifts off.

When we reminisce about the good times, we can talk without the shadow of addiction—free of the times of extreme stress and danger. We are outside the anger. We are transported by love towards more love.

Chapter 6:
Madeline Teresa
Carman Pia Ore Lubrano

The center of that big family, and our childhood, was Grandma Hammons. The Lord broke the mold when he made Madeline Teresa Carman Pia Ore Lubrano. Mere words cannot adequately capture her essence.

Pam and I would connect and roll our eyes when Grandma started yammering on in her first language.

Madeline Teresa Carman Pia Ore Lubrano was born and raised on the island of Malta. The insanely fun and ornery Grandpa, before he was a husband or father or grandpa, was stationed on the island of Malta in the Navy in 1954. Learning this as children helped us realize there is a much bigger world out there than our fifteen acres: Our parents and grandparents had had full lives before us.

Grandma was a combination of classy, sassy, hilarious, and impossible to understand. It wasn't her heavy accent that eluded us; it was not knowing what was going on in that mind of hers. We often had to translate what she was saying when someone couldn't understand her. She would then giggle and start speaking in Maltese and say to us in English, "Why not? They can't understand me anyway."

She had gorgeous features: thick dark hair, dark eyes, and olive skin. I often saw her rubbing her cute, round belly while giggling, and it was not unusual to catch her looking at herself in the mirror, hands on hips, of course speaking Maltese. She was as funny as she was mischievous. She marched to the beat of her own drum or, as Grandpa used to say, "beat the tune of her own drum." She had warm, soft hands. Her remedy for any internal illness was Metamucil. For external ailments, her go-to was Vaseline. Her cooking was awful. Luckily Grandpa prepared almost all the meals. Grandma loved to clean all the mattresses in the house. All. The. Time. She'd call for us grandkids to haul a mattress outside, where she would proceed to sweep it off with a broom and sometimes hose it off with water, after which it would take days to dry.

Her iconic red lipstick was part of her daily routine long before Taylor Swift embraced the look. Her ability to pull off wearing a pair of high heels with sweatpants and a Kentucky Derby-worthy hat, while sporting her bright lipstick—to Sunday Mass—is still legendary.

Her love for Jesus was rich, endearing, and practical. A print of the *Head of Christ* by American artist Warner Sallman hung near the front door in the living room of their home. I often sat in the reclining chair, her standing next to me, staring at that picture of Jesus and bursting out with the phrase: "Isn't he beautiful?"

Grandma moved slowly and methodically in everything she did. Even when we were running late to some event and were all piled in her 1980s brown Pontiac Phoenix—that she ended up spray painting because she wanted it a different color. Instead of rushing out the door like the rest of us, knowing darn good and well we were running late, she'd decide to vacuum the living room first. After she finished vacuuming the living room, she would step out on the front porch, place her hands on her hips, breathe the fresh air, and smile at us—completely oblivious to the frustration and panic plastered over all our faces. Despite the sense of urgency in our voices when she finally made it to the car, she still stalled, making the sign of the cross accompanied by the Trinitarian formula, putting on another coat of her red lipstick, fluffing her hair, adjusting the mirror, then backing out of the driveway at a speed that indicated we had absolutely no obligation to be anywhere. Once on the road, she'd suddenly accelerate as though the fire of her grandkids was finally lit under her butt. She drove faster than anyone else I have ever ridden with.

Her driving was in fact awful. She was party to more traffic stops than any one human should ever have in four lifetimes. They were often the result of driving down the left side of the road, since that is what she learned in Malta. She'd refuse to wear a seatbelt and, if stopped, proceed to try to convince the officer that she was not familiar with seatbelts or how to use them—because in Malta seatbelts were not required. This sometimes resulted in a warning, but officers started catching on and began issuing her tickets. She once got so many speeding tickets that she was thrown in jail, where she befriended the officers and even convinced them to make her a cup of tea: real European tea. This jail visit required her appearance in court, where she proceeded to stand after the judge entered and told everyone they could be seated. The judge asked her in a courtroom full of people why she was still standing. She simply raised her right hand and proclaimed in her Maltese accent, "I plead guilty." The courtroom erupted in laughter—even the judge.

Grandma often loaded a bunch of us into the car and took us to her favorite place in Kansas City, the Country Club Plaza. The Plaza is Kansas City's premier outdoor shopping and dining district, filled with romantic Moorish architecture, European art, and dazzling fountains. It's trendy, it's sexy, and it is a beloved location for Kansas City residents.

One trip, Grandma decided to treat us to some dessert at a café. We stood in complete awe of the variety of cheesecakes that filled the pastry case. We were so distracted by our options that we did not even notice when Grandma pulled a Ziploc bag full of change out of her purse. It was when she started counting out the change that we were mortified. "Grandma, what are you doing?" I asked. "I know you have cash in your purse!"

"Il-Madonna!" she exclaimed. "I had too much change at home and wanted to get rid of it."

She proceeded to pay the $7.59 tab all with coins.

She was fun and fair, and she was strict. She had a paddle with holes in it hidden in the front linen closet of her home. She wasn't playing around. Trying to keep fourteen grandchildren in line is not for the faint of heart. After we got a whoopin' on our backside, she'd make us sign it. Needless to say, it didn't take long for the paddle to be so full of names that it basically became a big blob of black permanent-markered signatures. As we got older, we got wiser and started hiding the paddle from her—but she just bought another one, and then another one.

One day, as I was nearing my senior year in high school, she was muttering in Maltese in the kitchen.

"Tricia"—which she pronounced *tree-sh-uh*—"come in here and sit down; I need to talk to you."

"Yes, Grandma." I made my way to the dining room table.

She put on another layer of red lipstick as I sat, wondering what could possibly be so important.

"Now listen, I need you to be serious for a moment because you're always joking and laughing. This is serious."

"Okay, Grandma. Are you sick?"

"You see what I mean. You never take me serious."

"Okay, Grandma, I am being serious. But what do you need to talk to me about?"

"Well, now that you have a boyfriend, I need to make sure you are being safe."

"Safe with what, Grandma?"

"Oh, *qalbi*. There you go again, not being serious. You know ... safe."

"Grandma, you don't have to worry about that. I've decided I'm not going to have sex until I am married," I said.

"Oh, who are you fooling? No teenager waits to have sex until they are married—and if they say they are, they are lying," she responded, giggling.

"No, Grandma, I'm serious, and this conversation is over. There's nothing to talk about. I am not having sex," I insisted, half smiling, half laughing.

"Tricia, if you are anything like your grandmother," she said, "there is no way you're waiting until you're married."

I stood away from the table. "Well, Grandma, this body is a temple, and I am not giving it to just anyone." I did a silly little dance resembling a half turn while I motioned my hands down the length of my body.

She started giggling and speaking in Maltese.

"Well, I must know: What do you do when you get the edge?"

For those who don't have a Maltese grandmother with a thick accent, that translates into, *What do you do when you get the urge?*

Intense laughter doubled me over. Grandma joined in. We both ended up in tears.

"Grandma, you're one of a kind and I love you. I promise, you have no worries." I leaned over and kissed her on her forehead.

In later years, I realized that Mom had inherited her own mother's zest for adventure and freedom, and that Pam and I had too. How that played out was unique for each of us.

Chapter 7:
The Big, Quieter,
Conservative German Family

Dad was one of five children. His family of origin was the quieter, more conservative family.

Pam and I were two of twelve grandchildren to our paternal grandparents. Their home was often filled with the sound from the sunroom of a football game on television, accompanied by the cheers of men. The laughter of women and kids in the kitchen indicated that a wild and crazy fast-paced card game of pounce was being enjoyed. Or Grandpa Barbarick at the table with his sons, drinking coffee, talking politics, and eating whatever wonderful treat Grandma Barbarick had made.

Pam and I often spent the night with my Dad's parents, and loved the time we spent with them. As we grew older, I spent more time with them than Pam did. My bond with them was the kind which comes with being the baby grandchild. Although they had a spare bedroom for us grandkids to sleep in, I always chose to sleep on their couch in their sunroom, in which a wood-burning stove reflected its orange glowing warmth on the TV screen and windows. We always awoke to Grandpa reading the Bible, and the dinging of Grandma's spoon as she stirred her coffee.

For a time, we lived just one pasture away from them. Regular visits included our annoying cousin, Ben—Peedy—who lived next door to us. We'd help Grandma pull weeds in her garden or pick veggies. Many a late summer's day was spent canning with her. We played thousands of rounds of the boardgame *Aggravation* while her favorite soap opera sounded in the background.

We would occasionally accompany Grandpa on a grocery delivery. Our grandparents had a room in their basement that was lined with shelves Grandpa had made to house the stacks of canned goods and produce you often find in a food pantry. My grandparents had a community food pantry in their basement where families often came to get food when they had fallen on hard times. Sometimes, Grandpa would take the food to families in need. He would ask us to ride along to help him deliver groceries. This was the birth of my love for helping others. We attended church with Dad's parents.

Members of this large side of the family included Aunt Judy and Uncle Dave, who lived in Arvada, Colorado, and who came home several times a year. Aunt Judy worked for Hershey's. For each visit, they would arrive with tubs filled with candy. It was Pam's and my job to arrange brown paper grocery bags for each family, so that the goods could be evenly distributed—which we did with the precision of a small-town baker weighing half ounces of flour in the pioneer days. Their visits were comparable to Christmas morning. They didn't have children of their own, but treated Pam and me as theirs. Growing up, we all took trips together to visit them in Colorado. It was a treat to see them and explore that beautiful state. Pam and I once even spent an entire week at a cabin in Breckenridge, where we were met with twelve inches of snow to play in for the week.

Back at Grandma and Grandpa's, one Saturday each year, our entire family tended to their stations in the unfinished basement of my grandparents' home where the annual meat cutting and packaging took place. Dad and the uncles purchased calves, raised them, and then butchered them to fill our freezers with meat for the year. This was one of my favorite traditions. The men would use a large meat processing saw to cut up the cows into their respective cuts. Some of the meat was passed to a few of my uncles, who ran it through a meat grinder to make one-pound packages of ground beef. Tables were set up as stations: one to wrap the meat, one to tape the wrapped meat, and one to write with black Sharpie what type of meat rested in those little packages of love. Around lunchtime, Grandma, Pam, and I would go upstairs and make fresh tenderloin sandwiches for all of us to enjoy on the long, rectangular tables that we set up around the house.

Grandpa Barbarick was a product of the Great Depression. His father left his mother—my great-grandmother—with five children. He even took the milk cow when he abandoned them. Grandpa's childhood was one of rural poverty. After our grandparents married, they lived in a one-bedroom home on a small plot of land that became a part of what later became the Barbarick Holler. This holler was a homestead comprised of four large lots, separated by two cow pastures between them. Eventually, my grandparents built a larger house on the property, and two of my uncles did the same. When Heath, Pam and I were children, Dad built our home where his childhood house had stood.

My wild Catholic mother inevitably started dating my Baptist father, a Jesus-loving German American, raised in that extremely conservative Baptist home. Their couple-ship was initially unacceptable to Dad's mother. Grandma had the best of intentions, but she felt that Baptists were not to marry Catholics. My mom and dad ignored her objections and dated throughout high school, making themselves husband and wife soon after graduation. My parents were madly in love—as a child, I never heard them fight.

When my parents married, Mom joined the Baptist Church with Dad. After they had Heath, then Pam, and then me, the church became a part of our lives too. We attended every week, with vacation Bible school every summer.

"Why can't we take a week off?" I would ask.

"God gives us seven days a week. We can sacrifice one morning for him." Dad must have repeated this thousands of times during my childhood.

He was a pillar of faith-based strength. Mom had her own deep faith too, but it was Dad who made sure our foundation was built around the church and the Bible.

As a small child in Sunday school, I was completely disinterested in the lessons, because those delivering the message did so with little to no enthusiasm.

The only Sunday Dad considered letting us skip was when the church invited Rosemary to sing. Rosemary was a short, older woman who considered herself the queen of opera in the church. Dad knew we would burst out laughing no matter how hard we tried not to. It didn't matter how much we prepared ourselves. Her voice was a hard-to-explain blend between opera-singing and howling at the moon.

The moment we knew she was in church, we'd start fidgeting in our seats to distract ourselves from what was about to take place.

The moment she would take the stage, my expression would change.

My siblings and I wouldn't dare look directly at one another, but out of the corner of my eye, I'd spy my brother grabbing his cheeks and mouth, then squeezing them in an attempt not to lose control. I'd start vibrating inside, trying with every ounce of strength not to make a noise. My entire body would start shaking as if I'd been left out in the cold. If only that were the cause. The shaking would continue, and I'd see my brother holding his face together, doing his best not to burst. And Rosemary wouldn't have even opened her mouth yet.

We'd get the stink-eye from our parents. It would do nothing to stop us.

I'd begin to giggle uncontrollably at Heath's contortion.

And then Rosemary would begin to sing, filling the sanctuary with a level of opera that threatened to blow out the stained-glass window of that small space. That's when everything would fall apart. Sometimes Pam would commit the cardinal sin of making that direct eye contact with me. Our giggling would then escalate into wails of laughter which could not be contained and which was indescribable. It would somehow manage to emerge from us one part high pitched, like a dolphin squeak, and one part silent. I would be laughing so hard that sound did not always come out, me doubled over and trying to conceal an emotional outburst that had a life of its own.

What it did accomplish was to create a domino effect. No one was immune—well, maybe Dad was. Mom would begin laughing while Dad would have to share his stink-eye beyond his children. Inevitably, our outburst would also get Grandma Barbarick going.

When we returned home, there'd be a spanking from Mom—even though she participated in the mirth. Her spankings for any of our missteps were almost always comically ineffective.

It's safe to say that Rosemary was not affected by our laughter, as she came back to sing many times throughout my childhood. So many times. If only we all had the confidence of sweet Rosemary.

※

I check my phone. It is after five. I down the root beer, gather up the blanket, and reimagine the recycling bin as a basket at which to aim my empty cup. "A two pointer!" I exclaim. I momentarily feel Pam's excitement inside my own, but then the weight of the years' worth of changes lands back on my shoulders, intent on burrowing into my heart.

Chapter 8:
Rx: Basketball Wisdom

The day after the brain surgery on Betsy, Pam and I ran through the woods seeking our next adventure. We stumbled upon the greatest treasure two girls, seven and nine, had ever dreamed of. Treasure to put the Beverly Hillbillies' riches to shame: a veritable mountain of aluminum soda and beer cans.

Our jaws dropped. Complete awe. We didn't speak a word. We'd struck gold. We ran home as fast as possible to gather as many trash bags as we could find. We were convinced we'd fill all of them. Back at Mount Tin Can, we dove in. Our eagerness could only be understood by amateur treasure hunters of all stripes. Giddy with excitement, we began to fill the bags with goods that, when cashed in, would allow us to buy cartons of Bonkers candy, rent endless Blockbuster movies, and possibly even purchase a new game for our Nintendo.

We hadn't even half-filled one bag when we each experienced piercing pain in our arms and legs. We kept piling in the cans. We ignored, as best we could, the pain. Then we heard them. Bees. We looked at each other and realized what had happened— we were surrounded by thousands of bees who were not happy at all at how we were dismantling their home. We ran home, screaming in pain. The only thing on our minds was escaping the little flying terrors and getting some relief from the stings. Pam went straight into the bathroom and found the toothpaste. She said she had read in the *Highlights* magazine—a standard in school in the 1980s—that toothpaste would take the sting away. Our parents came home from work to a house reeking of minty toothpaste and two girls covered in it.

The experience didn't affect our fearlessness. A few days later, we made our way back up to the mountain of cans to retrieve our treasure. Luckily for us, Dad had moved the beehive to a location that was safe for both us and the bees.

⁂

Fast forward from age seven to age twelve.

Pam and I stretched out on our backs on the grass of our back-yard, looking up at the stars, catching our breath from the two-hour, one-on-one basketball game we'd just finished. June had been exceptionally warm. Crickets chirped as a breeze rapidly cooled our sweaty skin, brushing over us. We lay in silence, soaking up the stars. The floodlight Dad had recently secured to the hundred-year-old oak tree highlighted the concrete slab for the half basketball court that he had poured for us. It was nearing 10 p.m. but, for a couple of preteens, this night of one-on-one basketball was still young. The back door of our home creaked open and we both tilted our heads toward the house, acknowledging Dad. "I'm going to bed, kids. Don't stay up too late, and lock the door when you come in," he said.

With that, Pam and I jumped to our feet, played a quick round of rock, paper, scissors to see who would get the ball, and started our next round of one-on-one.

⁂

This was our norm. Endless nights, bottomless basketball. If Malcom Gladwell's assertion is true that ten thousand hours of practice are required to become an expert, then Pam and I should have been playing in the WNBA by high school. Pam's unquenchable desire to be the best at any sport she played was evident in her commitment to practice in them. Basketball is just one example.

Alongside her unparalleled athleticism, Pam had the sweetest disposition. Her heart was so big, it's surprising it even fit into her small body. She was dedicated and positive. Sure, her competitive spirit got the best of her at times and could cause her emotions to overwhelm her rationality, but isn't that what competitors do? She was as kind and sweet as she was fierce.

As she got older, that fierceness took center stage. She wouldn't blink an eye to bodycheck someone on the softball field or deliver enough of an elbow in a basketball game to send a player flying. Our pastor had a saying that perfectly applied to Pam: "She was as gentle as a dove and as wise as a serpent."

I was already convinced that she was going to be a trailblazer as an adult. I had unwavering confidence that she'd be the country's leading brain surgeon, and the first woman president. She could do absolutely no wrong in my eyes. *Remarkable* is not an adequate word to describe what I thought of Pam.

She told me when she moved on up to middle school that she wouldn't be around to protect me, but that she'd taught me well. "You know what to do if someone picks on you, or if you see someone picking on someone else, right?" she asked one day.

"Yes, I know."

"Okay, well I didn't hear enough confidence in that voice, so tell me. I want to hear it."

"I make sure a teacher isn't looking, and I double up my fist and let them have it."

"That's right. You make sure you give them the best knuckle sandwich they have ever had and let them know they picked on the wrong girl."

"I know, but I wish you didn't have to go to middle school."

"Well, I am growing up and so are you. We'll be in the same school in a few years. But from now on, it's your job to stand up for yourself and others."

Pam's words of wisdom stuck because the next school year, I found myself dealing with the biggest kid in our school, who was also the biggest bully. I'd had enough. The previous year's pep talks from my big sister had birthed a sixty-pound bully-fighting machine. The bully was a big boy; I was at most half his size. This was a modern-day David and Goliath—except I wasn't armed with a stone. I only carried confidence the size of Texas. It was my first personal introduction to the Maltese women's blood running through my veins. That, and I wanted to make Pam proud. My temper flared and inflamed my complete disapproval of how he treated others. Combined, they landed me on top of this kid in the middle of the school's witch's hat—a sort of playground merry-go-roundish ride.

It was the best playground fight thus far of 1989; basically a reenactment of Ralphie's assault of Scut Farkus in *A Christmas Story*—gibberish, rage, and all. It didn't last too long, as the chants of all our classmates surrounding the witch's hat caught the attention of a teacher on recess duty. As my third-grade body was hauled off the bully, I mouthed to him, "This isn't finished."

The teacher who lifted me off the bully let out the occasional giggle while escorting me to the principal's office. After calming down enough to realize I was the one in trouble, I was struck with horror. *What have I done?* I had never been sent to the principal's office before.

The principal told me to have a seat in the hallway while he spoke with Mrs. Graham. The door to the principal's office shut, and I decided it was a good time to start drafting my eulogy on a scrap piece of paper that I told myself I had borrowed from the secretary's desk. It went something like this:

We gather to pay tribute to Tricia, a young girl who did more than simply show up to school to do schoolwork—she beat up bullies. She had a spirit that was competitive in the most jubilant of ways. Her ability to never stop talking was notated on every report card from the inception of her school career. Her ability to eat a grilled cheese sandwich without even biting into the bread was to be admired. Her hero was her big sister, Pam, even though Pam's words of inspiration were the reason for Tricia's life being cut short. Tricia's favorite hobbies included playing basketball for hours with her sister, shoveling as many watermelon Bonkers as possible into her mouth at one time, and crawdad hunting with her big brother.

My eulogy fantasy was cut short when the principal stuck his head out of his office to beckon me to either partake of my last meal or to discuss with me what took place in the witch's hat. I was prepared to offer my final words when I was catapulted out of my fear by a belly laugh. Not from me—from the principal. This incident marked a turning point in my life, and my fame for beating up bullies was born that day. Instead of ending my life, that principal offered me a high five and told me that was one of the greatest stories he had been told in his career, and to keep up the good work of keeping bullies out of our school.

Chapter 9: Nostalgia

The story of our childhood is not some daydream. We really were that close. Then we suddenly weren't. Now we are close again, but in a different way. We are bound by adult love and bonded through Allie. I am Pam's protector, yet she is still my teacher. The strange thing is, I have physical and legal freedom, while she has a whole lot of supervision and support. Her condition in one way deprives her of personal freedom, yet at the same time, allows her a form of captive dignity. She is not in jail—though she has been—yet she is also not driving a car, working at a job, nor living in her own place in any conventional type of life. What she has that we on the outside might envy is a steady routine, free from common worries that plague our days—no budgeting for meals and bills, scheduling our hours around changing responsibilities. Those considerations are taken care of for her.

However, her life as a resident wherever she lives is just as valuable as anyone else's, and her role without a formal job or career or family title is as important as anyone else in any other living situation. Until she could no longer carry on a conversation, she had friends and impacted others. Until she could no longer play those roles, she was a daughter and sister in our family.

Even under her current circumstances, she is a person. She is a woman. She has memories. She has hopes and dreams. Those hopes and dreams are sadly often buried under layers of shame. As I write, I don't avoid asking her about her favorite memories. She deserves to go back in time as much as any other person. Some of her stories overlap with mine, others are ones I haven't thought about for a while. I fill in blanks a lot of the time. The stuff she brings up and recalls is profound.

Chapter 10:
Life and Death

December 23, 1988: We were both freezing but still shooting hoops.

Mom's car came down the driveway; we could barely see the basketball, and Pam had just called, "Last basket wins." We stepped to the side, headlights blinding us—our basketball rim hung above the garage door.

The second Mom opened the door, and we moved in to hug her, we saw that she was crying. Pam asked her what was wrong.

She started off with, "Kids, something terrible has happened." Then she asked us to go inside. We hurried, silently, and took a spot on the couch. Mom called for Heath to join us. He sat next to us, and Mom couldn't even speak for a while, as she was crying so hard. Then she told us.

"Your cousin, Chad, passed away in a four-wheeling accident tonight." She went on to explain that our eighteen-year-old cousin had been out riding with our other cousin, Shaun, and some of Shaun's friends, and wasn't familiar with the area. "He ran into a cabled fence that runs across the City Lake Dam."

She managed to get it all out between sobs. We sat silently.

I was only in first grade, but I thought how terrible it must have been for my aunt and uncle and their boys, all visiting from California.

Mom asked us if we had any questions. She wanted to know how we were feeling, and then she said we must all go over to our grandparents' house because the whole family was going to meet there. She was unable to control her sobbing as she asked us to get bundled up.

When we piled into the car, Pam reached for my hand and held it tightly, and I squeezed hers, at which point she burst into tears. A chain reaction of tears began and continued for the fifteen-minute car ride.

The moment we entered the front door, I encountered a sadness I had never known before. Everything that followed that night seared its way into my child-brain.

To my eyes there were no longer any decorations adorning the house. Every last corner instead was filled with tears—a sense of suffocation by crying people. Pam and I were crying too. In the midst of it all, just as I felt like I could not breathe anymore, Pam grabbed my hand again and asked if I wanted to go outside. I told her, "Yes." She led me out to the front porch—an eight-year-old leading a six-year-old on her journey of grief.

We sat on the front porch, bundled up in our coats and stocking caps. Pam put her arm around my shoulder and started to cry again.

"Why do you think God took Chad so young?" she asked.

"I don't know," I answered.

"Well, I know he is in heaven, so he isn't sad like we are," Pam said.

I gave her a loose, "Yes." We sat quietly as we stared at the star-filled night. The moon was so bright that night that it lit up my grandparents' front porch; it was as though someone had turned a streetlight on.

"I think God made the moon so bright tonight to help us feel less sad," Pam remarked.

"I still feel sad." Tears streamed.

"Me too," Pam said.

"I feel really, really sad for Uncle Darrel and Aunt Janet," I continued, thinking some more.

"Me too. Not only did their son just die, but it's Christmas, which makes it extra sad," Pam said as she sniffed.

"Yeah, I don't know if I will ever stop crying," I said.

"Me neither," Pam said, trying to choke back tears.

We slid onto our backs on the porch so we could get a better view of the stars.

"Do you think people turn into stars when they die?" Pam asked.

"No. We go to be with God in heaven and get new bodies," I responded.

"So, you think Chad has a new body now?" Pam asked.

"Yes." It may have been a response from a young girl, but it was made with absolute conviction.

"What do you think heaven is like?" Pam asked.

"I don't know, but I imagine it is everything that makes us super happy on earth, times a million. The Bible says there are streets of gold and no sadness."

"Well, there's a lot of sadness here tonight," Pam noted.

"Yeah, there is."

"I don't want to go back inside. There's too much sadness," Pam said.

"Me neither. Let's stay out here," I suggested.

We stayed there lying on the porch until it was time to return home.

Chapter 11:
Sudden Changes

I was in my eighth year of life. Heath, Pam, and I had been running around our property like we always did, when we heard the hum of Dad's pickup as it came into range. It was unusual for him to come home early, thus the three of us ran to meet him near the garage, where he often parked. Mom pulled right up behind him in her station wagon, the one we'd recently taken a three-week road trip in from Kansas City, through Denver, then over to San Francisco and San Diego, and back home.

Pam jumped up into Dad's arms. Something told me to stand back and read the situation. Dad seemed distracted, and he didn't smile, even though he was holding Pam and looking over her at Heath and me.

Mom got out of her car, her makeup smudged. It was clear that she'd been crying. The next thing I knew, Dad and Mom were hugging Heath and Pam and me. They led us to the side of our house, where the roof of our garage met the ground. We often sat there to talk. They waited for the three of us to sit and then Dad told us, while Mom listened with tears in her eyes, that what he had to say was difficult—and that regardless of what we were about to hear, we were to remember he and Mom loved us more than anyone or anything else in the world.

My old empathic soul already knew what he was about to tell us.

"Your Mom and I have decided to divorce. This is in no way easy for us, and we want to make sure that the transition is as easy for you kids as possible."

I'd still never seen them fight. We were not aware they had any problems. What he told us was shocking. Heath and Pam began crying. I sat quietly with a million thoughts racing through my head.

Mom and Dad embraced us kids again, all at the same time, and, in the warmth and togetherness of that hug, I was both comforted and bereft. Mom was falling apart. I sensed that Dad was trying to stay strong for us but really wanted permission to fall apart too.

I knew in that moment, despite all my questions and confusion, that this was a decision that they had made and there was no trying to talk them out of it. I knew I especially had to be strong and accept the situation with no fuss, for the sake of my parents.

As Dad and Mom told us about the divorce, my young people-pleasing brain wasn't about to allow me to shed even a single tear, as it would only make my parents feel worse than I knew they already did.

❦

Our move to town was an easy adjustment for me because I kept telling myself it would be best for everyone if I helped make the whole situation work. I held in all of my emotions. Heath and Pam openly expressed their frustrations regarding the changes. Pam, especially, carried her heart on her sleeve.

I became the protector of Pam's heart, often distracting her so that she could cope with the transition. We were faced with the sudden dissolution of our idyllic childhood—and I wanted so badly to see to it that my big sister was okay. I was hyper-aware of her feelings, almost as though we were twins. Whenever I sensed her sadness around the move, I would wrap my arms around her and squeeze her tight and rest my head on her shoulder to let her know everything was going to be okay. I was a second-grader carrying the responsibility of everybody's happiness on my little-child shoulders. Everything was going to be okay because I was going to make it that way.

Our parents were intentional in their efforts to keep our routines as normal as possible for us. We were not bound to a strict parenting plan. They were flexible with their time with us. Because they navigated their divorce with us in mind, we did not feel restricted from seeing one parent in favor of the other. They chose to live less than a few miles apart, so we had the luxury of going to whichever house we wanted on any given night. We continued spending so much time with our grandparents and our extended family that I never felt deprived for time with either side. Our parents could give life lessons in co-parenting to other couples who are separating.

Dad moved into a small, red-brick home in town as a temporary measure while he built us a new home near his parents' place. There was a pullout couch in the living room which we'd all snuggle on to watch dramas, thrillers, and mysteries. The sofa was colored in orange and gold tones, featuring the repeated image of a rustic barn, complete with wagon wheel outside it—or was it a water wheel? The entire scene was surrounded by flowers and some birds that were either pheasants or turkeys. The fuzzy velour-type texture was scratchy against the skin—proudly representing a cultural phenomenon of its era.

Dad woke us early and warmed up some Svenhard's breakfast bear claws in the microwave, still wrapped in plastic, for our car ride to my grandparents'—as we'd go there in mornings to catch the school bus. I often ate Pam's share as she fell asleep on my shoulder. I was an early bird like Dad. One day, while we were still building the house, Dad took us to the Wonder Bread bakery outlet, aka the day-old bread store. The aroma of the bakery could be smelled miles away.

The sight of the loaves of bread and the snacks that lined the shelves made my mouth water. Hostess pies as far as the eye can see. My favorites were the Zingers and Twinkies. It truly was a place of snack-wishes come true.

Mom moved into our great uncle's rental property, a home with a distinct smell. Rich, dark wood panels lined every wall, and the carpet was teal. Appointed with cream-colored Formica countertops and honey oak kitchen cabinets, combined with yards of Laura Ashley florals that clashed with some of Mom's Southwestern art. The bathtub, toilet, and sink were pink.

I loved the location because it was directly across the street from the high school's football fields. Thus, every Friday night during football season, Pam and I would run across the street to hang out with our friends and watch a game.

Mom still worked as a home-health nurse for the senior living community—and would work a second job, typically in retail or at a restaurant—and Pam and I loved going to work with her every year on Bring Your Kids to Work Day. Her employer put on a day of fun activities, including one of the best picnics I have ever attended. The picnic tents went on forever with a culinary spread that included juicy burgers, hot dogs, and potluck-style sides that would melt in your mouth. The dessert station was what kids dream of, with everything from ice cream sundaes to cookies and cupcakes.

Pam and I always shared a bedroom. She was a night owl to my early bird, so her waking me with her flop into bed was the only thing I found irritating about her. The problem only worsened when Dad bought us a waterbed.

The outdoor activities we'd pursued at Heavenly Acres were simply relocated to town. When we weren't sleeping or in school, we mostly played basketball. We built forts at the Boy Scout camp near Kellogg Lake, and rode our bikes around town and to and from our grandparents' houses. We helped my grandma weed her garden and started spending more time with our cousins on Dad's side of the family.

Having to leave our beloved childhood farm behind us and move to town may seem tragic to some, but in my mind it was another kind of paradise, having access to more activities and more family. Decades later, I would still smell the cinnamon of Grandma Barbarick's kitchen and feel the peace that comes from knowing that home can have many different meanings.

As everyone adjusted to the transitions, Dad worked on the new house in the cluster of the Barbarick Holler family homes.

When Dad and our uncles were working on the house, Heath, Pam, and I would venture off to Kellogg Lake to go fishing. Fishing was Heath's favorite pastime, and he always invited Pam and me to go along with him.

Mom's parents were a quick bike ride or walk across the main highway—in reality, a very small two-lane road that went through town, but busier than the other roads. Pam and I often ran back and forth between our grandparents' homes, sometimes dropping in to use the bathroom, grab a soda, or munch a snack before we were back on our bikes exploring town.

Chapter 12:
The Sports Queen

Afterschool sports activities took center stage September through June for Pam. On the court or field, she moved through and around opponents as if she'd practiced any given move a thousand times. Sometimes, on the basketball court, I couldn't even see her feet touch the ground, her movements were that quick. On the softball field, playing with lightning reflexes and fierce determination, she commanded the game from behind the plate, crouched low like a warrior ready for battle. As a catcher, she's the heart of the defense. Sometimes, I didn't recognize certain people in the stands; people who didn't even have children would come to see her play. As is characteristic of a top athlete, Pam was motivated, passionate, disciplined, persistent, committed, competitive, confident, coachable—and always the team leader. The sound of celebrations followed her; always a crowd of friends, including new ones, around. *The life of the party,* many said. It didn't stop there: The As on her report cards were also stacked in a neat column.

Pam instilled in me a love for University of Kansas basketball at a young age. We spent many nights watching their games, especially during March Madness—an intense array of college and university tournaments over a short time. We often wore the only KU item we owned: the now vintage 1990s University of Kansas kangaroo-style pullover puffer jacket. Pam said their program's first coach was the inventor of basketball and she could talk for hours about Kansas's exceptional history in sports.

We'd study the players; we knew their names, numbers, and heights. We enjoyed the pleasure of watching some of the best players in the Jayhawk program play in person—including Xavier Henry, Kenny Gregory, Raef LaFrentz, Paul Pierce, Drew Gooden, and Nick Collison. Our love of KU and the game helped keep us connected even after things began to fall apart.

The summer I turned twelve—1994—Pam and I played in the same softball league: hours of practicing and playing catch and taking turns pitching to one another. That was the summer we were nearly undefeated. I could feel the ball leave the pitcher's hand when I was on the mound. I intuitively also knew exactly when to swing to get the homerun—Pam affirmed this.

The softball fields were located at the bottom of the grassy hill where fans and spectators watch from lawn chairs, or from blankets on the grass. Pam was fearless on the field, taking every opportunity to steal bases. She intentionally placed herself in the middle of the hot box because she was so confident. Watching her make things happen out there put me under a spell. I spent much time and effort in every game studying her every move as she methodically ran bases and captured the adoration of the crowd with her out-of-the-park homeruns. I absorbed as much as I could to be just like her, but I was always outshone. It did not bother me.

These times could become otherworldly, like in the movie *The Sandlot*, where the whole gang played their only night game of the year as the fireworks lit the sky on Independence Day: Ray Charles singing "America the Beautiful," and the narrator talking about them feeling like they were playing in the big league under those lights, but baseball was still a game, except for the kid named Benjamin Franklin Rodriguez, for whom it was life.

Pam still has her KU jacket, which is now considered vintage.

Chapter 13:
New Family Dynamics

Sunday morning. I was a normal thirteen-year-old slowly emerging from the depths of slumber. I smiled at the soft sunlight filtering through my window blinds, casting gentle patterns on the walls. The familiar sound of Dad singing, and the faint sound of the radio, began to seep into my awareness. The aroma of pancakes reached my bedroom, signaling that it was not a school day.

I felt the warmth of the two comforters I always slept with. I contemplated whether I wanted to get up or fall back to sleep, when Dad's footsteps padded down the hall. I smiled as I anticipated what would take place on the provisional music stage that was my bedroom. My door swung open with a force that bounced it back off the door stop. Dad appeared at the threshold; he was holding the spatula as a microphone and belting out a passionate, *"Go, tell it on the mountain, over the hills and everywhere; go, tell it on the mountain, that Jesus Christ is born."*

His voice then transitioned to mimic Louis Armstrong. As I started giggling, Dad leaned over and kissed my head to wish me a good morning and let me know that the pancakes were almost ready. He then turned and danced out of my bedroom as he continued singing his hymn. His voice faded as he made his way down the hall, back to the kitchen where he had been preparing our Sunday morning traditional feast.

A man filled with joy, his voice was magnificent; the texture of his singing voice, velvet. His singing was ethereal and transported me to a place of peace.

❧

This delightful and cherished wakeup was one of Dad's traditions. Just a few weeks prior, the girls at church had begged Dad to sing the Leroy Van Dyke "Auctioneer" song. He bloody killed it.

Second to his singing voice, he was known for his humor: not in a dad-joke kind of way; just plain funny. Any time of day we could find ourselves laughing: sometimes calculated, and sometimes just with pure, spontaneous wit.

These sacred expressions of joy became unexpected issues for me.

❧

In 1994, after dating for a few months, Dad married Jeri, and she became my stepmom. I was now fourteen. I immediately gained another older brother, plus a six-year-old sister, Megan.

The brother was not around much, and I barely got to know him at all. I fell head over heels in love, though, with my new little sister, adoring the idea of having one. We bonded instantly. Megan, the lolly to my pop: pleasing in general, delightful. She made life much sweeter with her spirit. And of course, a lollipop is a small piece of sugary sweet candy. Also fitting.

Megan always greeted me with the greatest enthusiasm when I returned home from somewhere. Her sweet smile lit up a room. As a small child, she loved fiercely and had the kindest heart.

Megan's best friend was a lovely little boy, Logan. Everyone in our community loved him, but nobody did so as deeply as Megan. Logan had cerebral palsy and used a wheelchair. He loved red Converse high tops and sported a pair every day. Megan loved him with a fierceness I had never before seen in a child so young. His parents were dear friends of our family. Whenever they brought Logan over, he and Megan played together for hours. She included him in every way imaginable and took loving care of him. They were inseparable besties.

Megan became a new sidekick to me, and I loved every minute of it. We spent lots of time at Grandma and Grandpa's, playing board games or helping Grandma cook, work in the garden, or can goods.

She was my little shadow for years. I loved telling her the most extravagant bedtime stories filled with castles and princesses and underwater worlds that could only be accessed by the magical dolphin who we, as characters, befriended. There were also tiny fairies who swept us away from our backyard to new kingdoms. My stories transported Megan to lands full of unknown and undiscovered animals and plants. It was our secret place where we were so special that the kings and queens of these kingdoms considered us distinguished travelers and invited us to dine with them, which we'd do before returning to our homeland.

I was finally the big sister, and I took that role very seriously. I intended to be as good a big sister for Megan as Pam had been for me. I'd had the greatest teacher.

When Dad and Jeri married, Heath and Pam decided to move in full time with Mom. That was a tough pill for Dad and me to swallow. Heath was almost an adult, so his decision was his; we knew he'd move again soon to be his own person. It didn't mean we didn't still see each other, especially Pam and me, as we had school and sports and our sister bond. It did, however, change the dynamic.

Mom had more liberal rules at her place. She was the kind of mom who believed in letting kids be kids. She blasted Fleetwood Mac while dancing around the house, and never met a rule she couldn't bend. With feathered hair and too much Paul Mitchell hairspray, she embodied the carefree spirit of the '80s: more best friend than authority figure, raising her kids with a mix of love, laughter, and laissez-faire parenting. Boundaries were loose, supervision was light, and freedom was abundant. She trusted the world to shape her children just as much as she did.

As she became a single mom, she started exploring the types of freedoms that she hadn't had as a young, married woman with small children. Mom was a hard worker, often holding multiple jobs to help provide for her kids. When she wasn't working, and when we weren't together at our grandparents', she was out dancing the night away on the weekends. Pam often had the house to herself, and it became a perfect opportunity for her to entertain a new group of friends.

Heath spent less time with us. He grew up and if he wasn't fishing, he was on call as an EMT with the local fire department. He didn't waste a moment after graduation before enlisting in the United States Navy, trading small-town streets for the open sea in service to something bigger than himself. His thoughts were laser-focused on his own future now, not on us. Suddenly, we had a much older brother whose sights were set on military service. He prepared to leave for that role.

For me, life with Dad was still great, but life in Dad's house became difficult. I maintained a positive attitude and wanted the best for all of us as a new family. Jeri had a tough time adjusting to the easy, fun-loving relationship Dad and I had. He and I laughed a lot and could be super silly together. She found it challenging to fit into the carefree, Jesus-loving, silly household. No matter what I tried to do, Jeri neither approved of nor appreciated it. When she got irritated with me for reasons neither she nor I could explain, I still kept my rose-colored glasses firmly on my face. I tolerated the tough stuff because I loved my dad and Megan. I tried not to let it get to me—but at times it did.

Megan's own birthfather wasn't around much. It was easy and natural for Megan to call my dad, *Dad*. I loved that she did. It made us even more like sisters. Over time, it became obvious that Dad was unhappy with Jeri, but his commitment to giving Megan a strong foundation won out.

With Pam now living at Mom's, and as she began hanging out with other friends, I started to focus more of my time on making my own friends outside of the family. One day, in seventh grade, I was sitting in Mr. Savage's English class when the cutest girl with blondish-red, curly hair and hazel eyes randomly became my best friend.

"Hey, do you want to come over Friday night and spend the night?" Nicole asked.

"I'd love that!" I replied.

Nicole became my rock, and I hers. From that moment when she invited me to stay over, we were inseparable. We bounced back and forth between our houses for slumber parties, we now attended all the school functions together, and we joined each other on family vacations that year. Nicole talked me into joining the swim team with her—a sport that became a major part of my life. Also, importantly, a sport where Pam was not present. We laughed and had fun. Plain bagels with strawberry cream cheese—that's the stuff our days were made of.

To Nicole, I was *Tricia*, not *Pam's sister*. We walked around town with our group of friends, toilet-papered her house on Halloween night, and sneaked Grandpa's smokes. One time, we moseyed around the neighborhood trying to sell my grandmother's trinkets so we could go to McDonald's.

We'd get dressed up and go out for an evening of jazz whenever Nicole performed as the best saxophonist in our community. We got to be kids together, then teens—and forged a bond that helped me develop my sense of self-identity.

We have remained friends and have kept that strong bond.

Although Pam and Heath moved out of Dad's house when I was twelve—Pam fourteen, Heath eighteen or nineteen—we still spent a lot of time together given the joint custody, the closeness of our homes, and the flexibility of our parents and their post-divorce relationship.

When we first lived apart, Pam and I still played softball together in the summer league. I was grateful for that connection because even though we got to see each other when we overlapped time at Mom's or at our grandparents' homes, it wasn't the same. The basketball court at Dad's sat unused. Our once inseparable bond didn't feel as secure. I began spending more time with my German grandparents, whereas Heath and Pam appeared more centered at our Maltese grandparents'.

The second summer of living apart, Pam and I played on different softball teams because of our ages.

Pam started high school while I remained in middle school. Although Pam and I were two years apart in age, we were three years apart in grades. Suddenly, differences appeared in our likes, wants, and needs. By her junior year, Pam was being recognized for her athleticism and records. Athletic scholarship offers were already starting to flow in. Her friendships remained numerous and varied. Popularity in our community was measured not by *what* you knew but by *who* you knew; Pam was the who. Even with all her demanding sports schedules, she stayed strong in academics and continued with her aspiration of becoming a surgeon. Yes, the brain surgeon.

I watched her excel and believed that although she was academically brilliant, professional sports would win out. Sports were her first love. Everyone around her said they knew she'd be playing softball in college—and though many colleges would want her, I always saw the University of Kansas as her first choice. She was the epitome of the well-rounded student who simply had all her ducks in a row. I could have been envious of her, except that her success made it easy for me to be accepted without trying, just by virtue of being her younger sister.

Part Two:
Building Thunderheads

Chapter 14:
A Different Person

I was starting high school, and Pam was a senior. I was still living at Dad's, but still often spending the night at Mom's, with Pam. Pam's sleep habits were one of the first things I noticed that had changed since we had lived together full-time.

First it was one day, and then another, that she wasn't ready for school. She'd just stay in bed.

Next, her smile and energy disappeared. It was like all the enthusiasm she had had for learning had just drained out of her. I knew her marks were down because Mom and Dad talked about it. Her teachers had been in touch to let them know she seemed to suddenly be inexplicably falling behind.

When I asked her how she was doing, she'd snap at me.

Her quick-to-anger attitude replaced the usual gentle and loving Pam.

I found a bag of weed in her room. That was against the house rules, and against everything we'd been taught. I wasn't afraid for her; I was mad at her. This was not my Pam.

I concluded that she was turning destructive and selfish. I was furious that she was throwing everything away for what I assumed was just weed. It was incredibly stupid.

I myself was never tempted to try it. Even if my personality type were inclined, the drastic changes and negativity I saw in Pam were huge turn-offs.

With Heath heading to serve in the military, and Mom working multiple jobs, Pam had the house to herself a lot. She quit cleaning her room, and started leaving messes everywhere. She wore the same clothes over and over again, and stopped doing her laundry. She trashed Mom's house more than once. So many times, I'd go over and the whole place would reek of weed and cigarette smoke. In all fairness to Mom, she probably believed Pam's actions were a teenage phase. We all did.

Pam's new friend group cruelly mocked me, calling me self-righteous because of how involved I was in church. Any time Pam and her friends were at Mom's it was dark—in more ways than having the lights turned off. More than once, I found them doing different kinds of drugs and watching pornography. They didn't want me there, so it didn't take much to get me to want to leave.

I didn't like talking about hard things but preferred to ignore them. My parents simply didn't know what was going on or what we were up against. They both seemed hopeful that this would pass and she would come out on the other side.

I started to spend less time at Mom's. The times I was there, Pam focused completely on herself and never asked about me. Things shifted again when she began to steal my things from Mom's and Dad's houses. I never again saw the things that went missing, so I guessed she had sold them to get money for drugs. This happened a lot, which led to fights. And I was a fighter. We were both fighters. We'd get physical—knock-down, drag-out fights. I was approaching six feet in height, and although she was a lot shorter than me, she had more muscle. Had. Her physical condition was no longer that of a peak athlete. I was wiry and healthy. What she had over me in weight and width, she had lost to lethargy.

Pam's love for life and of life dimmed—she didn't even go to watch games anymore. I knew these weren't good signs, but none of the adults in our lives seemed to know the first thing regarding what to do about her situation. Most notably, our family did not deep dive into the emotional or philosophical of any of it.

At first, Pam's behavior may have been written off as a phase, a rebellion, being a teenager. When it didn't just stop—and later as it escalated—people began to whisper. People who'd raved about Pam's talents and skills were now distancing themselves. We'd come as a set, really, almost as if we'd been mismatched twins. But now I was not riding her coattails anymore. There were no longer victories to celebrate. I felt people start watching me, wondering, *Is she next?*

Just as there had been no stopping her in stealing bases, scoring points, and going above and beyond in sports and academics, there was now no curbing her drug use. It was as though she'd applied her determination and extreme participation to a new area—a very dangerous one.

Every week shifted her further into stranger status; there were no longer hey-theres or high-fives, only a gruff version of the voice she'd once had. When she did speak, she now swore. She became rough around the edges. I no longer recognized her.

I did not know what to call it, but I was in shock. I was upset, confused, and angry ... and scared. How could this have happened to someone so brilliant? How could this have happened to someone I loved?

She quit all her sports. Anything she did now was done in secret. She spun a web of concealment around her activities and fell deeper and deeper into its tangle.

She didn't want me around, and I started not wanting to be around her. It broke my heart in ways I could not vocalize. Distraught because I couldn't do anything to bring her back, I stayed away as much as possible. When we did stay in the same house after her decline, she was really just hanging about, drooped over the sofa, snapping at me for walking by. She smelled bad. Not just of weed, but the scent of the unclean: body odor on unwashed clothes. Whichever family member delicately and caringly broached the topic of hygiene with her, or whoever tried to broach subjects of motivation or goals, she shut them out. When the stars were aligned perfectly, Mom alone could cajole her into the shower.

I worked on just being Tricia at school. What was once cool—being Pam's sister—became embarrassing. I worried that everything I did would be judged by the new Pam. I stopped mentioning her at all. Still, the connection remained in their minds. It was a small town. People remembered everything. Her teachers even began asking me why I thought her grades were dropping.

Mom and Dad continued to live in the haze of *It must be a phase*, or perhaps they hoped and prayed it was. Many were probably convinced that Pam's passion for academics and sports would overrule whatever it was that she was going through.

Chapter 15:
Pachyderms

Pam, or rather, Pam's issue, was the elephant in the room. By the time the family began to realize its seriousness—that this wasn't just some phase—there was a whole herd of elephants making their home in Mom's house. They'd also started to mull around in Dad's. We started talking more, but didn't know what we were up against. My parents were doing the best they could with what they knew. They were loving and hard working but unprepared for the silent storm their child was facing. In our small corner of rural Kansas City, addiction and mental health weren't part of everyday conversation. There wasn't a platform, no real language for what was happening—just a quiet gap between love and understanding. Mom and Dad weren't avoidant; they were simply uneducated on this topic, like so many others in a time and place where those struggles stayed hidden behind closed doors.

Once we started talking about what was going on, everyone suddenly tried to get involved.

It started being discussed first by Mom's family: Being the loud and involved group that they were, this was natural. Shockingly to me, it started being talked about in Dad's conservative family's side, too. Importantly, although her addiction became a regular topic of family conversation, three things never happened: The first was that Pam was almost never involved in the talks in a meaningful way. They talked *about* her, not *to* her. This built her resentment, and she spent more time away from home. The second was that we did not try to learn what kinds of drugs she was using, nor via what route, nor how frequently. And the third was that we did not, as a whole, educate ourselves about addiction. Nobody had ever taught us how to navigate a serious problem like this.

I was so angry with Pam that I simply chose to not engage much—either with her or with our family discussions. I coped via avoidance. I was embarrassed to have teachers, administrators, and even people in our community constantly asking me what was going on with Pam. I wanted to crawl in a hole and disappear. I wanted to be *me*. I wanted them to ask about me, not my sister.

Therapy and counseling were also not things my family considered for any of us. As far as I know, I was the first of us to later intentionally pursue psychological counseling for myself. It was not necessarily frowned upon, just not really considered an option. Our Christian faith may have had something to do with this, with prayer being seen as an alternative to professional psychology and psychotherapy. Perhaps it was even considered a slight to God because it might offend Him that psychology could be as effective, or more, than prayer. There was a semi-prevailing opinion that the two—counseling and religion—could not be pursued together.

It was only decades later that people within churches began to see that while they believed God could heal, and has healed, we sometimes also need the assistance of skilled counselors to help us understand ourselves and others better. Some churches, including the one I would come to attend, would later have a counseling center. God gave us prayer; He also gave us wisdom of the human mind.

Chapter 16:
Diagnosis

Near the beginning of my sophomore year in high school, the family planned a trip to Chicago because Heath was graduating there as a new recruit for the United States Navy. My parents, a few aunts and uncles, Pam, and I all took this road trip, caravan style. Pam and I rode with Dad, Jeri, and Megan.

As usual, we had the radio on—singing in the car was a must. Between the songs, the DJ chatted about the song and took breaks for the weather report or a bit of news.

"That guy, he knows where I live and is gonna hurt me," Pam said, about one of the reporters.

We let it go. She rambled on about other people wanting to get her.

Not much of what she said made sense. We tolerated her on the ride there, changing the subject, redirecting the conversation, generally trying—with a silly song or a great story about Heath—to keep things positive and focused on him.

When we'd hit a bump in the road, she'd startle, and when a car with a broken muffler passed us, she placed her hands over her ears.

Dad asked her to close her eyes and try to nap. She could not. Her hypervigilance and borderline paranoia sucked the trip's joyful purpose out of the car. At some points I just wanted to shove her and tell her to smarten up, that we'd had enough of her, but instead I kept myself occupied by focusing on the celebration ahead and on being happy for Heath.

Pam could not do that. She couldn't sleep in the car, nor did she manage to sleep in our hotel room. Her paranoia about strangers was on repeat. She seemed to pace all night—at least when I awoke at various times, that's what she was doing.

The next day was filled with Chicago-style pizza, the Navy Pier, and watching Heath graduate. I was so proud of my brother and impressed by his new and distinguished stature. I had watched him leave for boot camp as my goofy, protective brother and now saw him as a United States Navy Corpsman. In that moment, I wasn't just proud; I was in awe. I was so occupied by being proud of him that I was able to finally stop thinking about some of the ridiculous things Pam had been doing.

The trip had been planned to last four days, but on day two, Dad pulled me aside and said he was so concerned by Pam's behavior—mainly some of the things she was saying—that he had decided we must leave to go home and get Pam to a hospital. We loaded up the car and headed back to Kansas City.

It was an awful ride: none of Dad's singing, no banter. I could tell by his furrowed brow and intense focus on the road that he was processing the challenges ahead. When we reached the city, we didn't even turn off for home; Dad headed straight for the hospital.

After a spell in the waiting room while Pam was being examined, the doctor told us that Pam's behavior over the last couple of days had been due to drug withdrawals.

Another result of that hospital visit was that, shortly afterwards, Pam also received a separate but possibly related diagnosis of bipolar disorder.

We were shattered to the core.

Pam's mental health plummeted after the diagnosis. She started to either not be home a lot, or to sleep and do practically nothing except stay in bed. Basically, she alternated between these two states: physically not in the house, or not being actually present when she *was* in the house. On the occasions when she did talk, it was a paranoid-fantasized type of conversation where she thought people were against her. Out to get her. People like me.

During the next stage of Pam's life, Heath was stationed in South Korea, and ended up serving on the frontlines of the war in Afghanistan. He had so much to celebrate with his career. We didn't know how to break the news to him about Pam and her ongoing battle with addiction.

When my parents finally did call him, he argued that it must be something else—that the doctors were mistaken. He said we were probably blowing her issues out of proportion. I understood Heath's reaction—he was away fighting a battle that would deeply impact his own mental health. He likely wasn't ready to take on this battle at home. We wouldn't have believed Pam's change ourselves had we not witnessed it.

It was only on his visit home, when he saw her again and attempted to converse with her—that Heath believed us. In their conversation, she showed disinterest, slurred her words, and could not finish sentences. He was distressed over it all, including how she was no longer showering or otherwise caring for herself. It had to have been a shock for him. We saw her daily, so the change for us had been gradual, and we were accustomed to her. He'd not seen her for months, so, for him, the change was striking and instant.

Years later, he would share with me that he'd revived Pam from an overdose shortly after returning from a deployment.

Pam continued to sneak around and take things from me. She stole anything she thought she could sell or trade: clothing, electronics, and CDs. I'd have freely given her everything I owned, but that was not how it went down. Some other entity possessed my sister now. We could feel it present when she was under the influence, as a dark force or presence or energy. It scared me. I distanced myself from her and her life. I angrily blamed her for hurting our parents and for having squandered her gifts and potential. Pearl Jam's song "Life Wasted" summed up my new feelings about Pam.

It was a miracle when she graduated high school.

Even after Pam received her formal diagnoses, we were not sure how to proceed. Mental health was not a topic at the forefront of any agenda in small-town Missouri. Nor was it something our family had prepared for, given our idyllic foundation, faith-based lifestyle, and close-knit relationships. If we'd been asked what we knew about drug use prior to Pam's decline, we'd have had nothing to say. Even after the diagnoses, we still had nothing. We were not educated on this topic. Had we been, given Pam's predisposition or susceptibility, we likely still wouldn't have been able to help.

I didn't want to be part of the conversations about Pam's mental health struggles and newfound addiction. The pain felt too heavy, the details too overwhelming. I preferred to stay on the sidelines, focusing on school, sports, and anything that offered a sense of normalcy. Mom and Dad kept the difficult discussions between themselves, shielding me from the emotional weight they carried each day. It wasn't avoidance; it was survival, for all of us, in the only way we knew how.

Starting in my childhood and early teen years, I was the kind of prematurely semi-adult girl who behaved like a leader, a parent, and a guide. Those roles I knew. With Pam's issues, I did not know how to handle my new role because I did not realize I had to fulfil a new role. I had no name for this thing. I watched my parents sink further into their worry and guilt while I witnessed Pam fall deeper and deeper into an unsustainable lifestyle. I never believed she was beyond recovery, but I did not really know what recovery was. How could I have? I was not some experienced and worldly adult—yet I found myself increasingly taking on adult roles. Recovery is different for each person, but nobody was there to teach me that.

⁂

In my Junior and Senior year, after Pam had graduated, I fully tore off my little sister badge and threw it in the trash. I focused on being a sister to Megan, not Pam.

I was so angry with Pam for different reasons. Her issues were causing me to stop looking forward to going to school. I tried to figure out ways to blend in and not be seen, but I was already six feet tall. Fortunately, no matter how many times I wished I could start fresh at another school where no one knew Pam, I knew I at least had my group of friends. What I did not realize was that I also had me.

And I really did have me. I had remained positive and caring toward others—also filled with ideas and energy to be a successful student.

During this time, I began pouring my energy into my church's youth group—a place that quickly became my refuge. What started as a way to stay busy turned into a calling. I eventually stepped into a leadership role, guiding younger teens while deepening my own faith. I joined mission trips, served the elderly in our community, and found healing in the act of helping others. It gave me purpose when everything at home felt too broken to fix.

I now started to answer inquiries about how Pam was doing with, "I don't know." It was an honest answer because, on the home front, Pam would disappear for weeks at a time. We didn't know either where she was, nor who she was with. The stress and turmoil this caused my parents changed our entire family dynamic.

We no longer spoke to one another the same way as we had. There was an ever-present undercurrent of fear, worry, concern. Our energy was consumed by Pam's issues, so we had little left to share with one another.

I grew scared. I had no idea if what had happened to Pam could happen to me. I knew I wouldn't use drugs, but I did not know if my body's genetics might cause my brain chemistry to break down the way hers had, even without them.

I didn't talk to my parents about those fears or any of my feelings—to me, it would have been selfish, given how Pam needed their entire focus. Even when she wasn't around, their attention was on her issues and trying to solve them, or on picking up pieces, or on pleading and bargaining with her to accept help.

No amount of prayer had helped either, nor was it comforting to me to think she was in God's hands. God surely couldn't be any part of this. I tapped down all my emotions again, not wanting to upset anyone. Pam needed help. Whether she accepted it or not, we kept trying. I kept trying until I knew I would disappear under the crushing weight of it all—all the trying to help, all the being concerned, all the whispers, all the *What happened to that star?*, all the *Something had to have happened for her to change*. All the theories—unspoken, discussed, or gossiped about—kept that dark cloud above our family. They maintained us in a perpetual state of looking up and waiting for the worst, paired with trying to look through it to see God waiting to part the cloud and announce we were dreaming.

Many who'd followed Pam's high school career had been elated at the prospect of following her college career. They had seen her as a trailblazer for their own young athletic and academic children. In essence, our entire community was in shock over the changes they saw in her. The neighborhood buzz around Pam playing ball in college was soon replaced by a community with a lot of questions, and that wanted answers. Also by some who made a lot of judgments. I fielded the former and turned away from the latter, not knowing either how to defend Pam or protect myself.

Chapter 17:
Curiosity

"I was thinking about our grandparents," I say. "Their homes."

"Those plastic covers on the furniture!" Pam laughs. "Was that brutal or what when you slept on them? The plastic would stick to you, so when you got up, it felt like your skin was peeling right off."

Now I'm laughing too. "The car rides with Grandma …"

"I can't believe we survived!"

When our laughter dies down, I suddenly have to know. "Did you have any thoughts about … well … you know, that things could change so much? I mean—"

"I know what you mean. Signs? Toots, I was a little kid. I was freewheeling and free-throwing—just like you."

"People want tidy packages; people want reasons. If there was something that happened that their loved one never shared, that explained the drug use—it could remove some of the guilt."

"By *people*, you mean *you*. You want reasons."

"Not just me. I've been doing a bunch of work—you know that. Trying to figure out what's needed, put into place what I discover is needed for help to be provided. Advocacy."

I think about what I've learned over the years I've been piecing together her story, but I still haven't asked Pam if there was something that I don't know about, maybe that she's been afraid to tell me. Sure, I know that many people will say there were no signs when it happened to them. Their loved one just started down a path that seemed like a phase; then, the next thing they knew, it was more than a phase, and it seemed too late to be reversed. People have said it runs in their family. What I have learned is they're right, but it's larger: Addiction runs in the human family, not just theirs.

"Earth to Toots. Hey, Tricia!" Her voice startles me.

"Sorry, I think I'm writing this book in my head."

"What is your head writing now?"

"How everyone is susceptible. That addiction doesn't discriminate. How people on the street are treated so badly compared to those who are not and yet ... well, a person taking cocaine in their mansion's marble suite endures the same craving as a person in a public washroom. Call it *high-bottom* instead of rock-bottom if you like. But we are all just one family."

"What else?"

"You're still pretty perceptive, PK," I say, my eyes narrowing slightly. "You know when I've got something on my mind."

She's adamant. "Spill it."

"I'm thinking about us. And others. Like, yes, there are high-risk situations: children growing up around parents who are using drugs—selling too, who are in gangs, kids entered into prostitution by their own families. But we weren't those families. There are other teens who suffer some kind of trauma, who turn to drug use as a way to cope—like their drug use is a symptom of coping but then contributes as much to the problem as the trauma does."

"I've met some people who've grown up with trauma or in the lifestyle, for sure. But I don't remember the story of everyone

I've met. I barely remember yesterday." Do I detect a tinge of irritation in her voice?

"I'm not asking you to remember and account for those people. I just wanted to ask you, well,"—*How do I put this?*—"if there was anything you've not told me. Did someone hurt you before you started using drugs?"

I am implying, I am fishing for some detail such as an assault followed by a consequential secret. Something she'd held back for the last thirty years because she didn't want me—or anyone else—to know.

"Like I'd have not told you something if there was something."

"But if you haven't, I can take it." I'm trying to reassure myself as much as I'm trying to reassure her. "We've been through so much together, I guess I want a reason. Even after all these years, I want a formula that makes sense. Something I can then say to the world: 'Hey, this is what happens and how it all works.'"

"I can tell you exactly what happened to me."

I brace myself. For shock.

"Curiosity."

My inner voice screams an elongated "Nooooooo!" If it were that simple, if addiction were that powerful, then everyone and anyone could become addicted. I could become addicted. My daughters could. My brain kicks in and tells me I already know that anyone can be addicted. I already said that the entire human family is susceptible. I need a more concrete reason that I could easily tell people to eliminate from life. Curiosity is not that reason. Curiosity is a good thing.

"Curiosity." Pam comes at me again with that good word. A word that is associated with great discoveries and inventions. "I never knew that wondering-and-trying would take over my whole life until it had. Nothing I'd previously been curious over had held that kind of power."

"Curiosity?"

"That's what started it. Yes."

"Give me a moment to process this."

"It's simple. I was curious. I tried. And then a part of me could not stop even when I wanted to."

I'm gonna need more than a moment.

I want a breakthrough reason—even though Pam had suffered significant brain damage, even though her body was ravaged with illness, with no way of undoing any of it, I still want to tie it up into a neat package. A cause, even if no cure is possible. Even if she has entire weeks now where she cannot string together complete sentences.

Imagine if she'd disclosed something that solved the mystery of her initial drug use. Imagine the dramatic ending for the book that gave the reason for Pam's addiction.

Curiosity. That's all it took.

"Oh my heavens. Curiosity."

Every one of us is susceptible to addiction if it can be triggered by curiosity. We encourage curiosity in our children. It's how we grow, how we choose careers; it's the precursor to innovation. Once again, it is confirmed for me—through that conversation—that although some of our loved ones may be more predisposed than others to the psychological pull of some chemical substance or other, we are all, in the end, susceptible. It only took curiosity to hook Pam for life.

I believe her. But what does my belief even matter now? We're decades into her addiction. Yes, we. As I am part of her life, her burden is my burden. Reasons matter. Her admission means that—with the proliferation of ever more dangerous chemicals on the streets, with their combinations that are more powerful and more addictive than previous iterations—the curious and vulnerable are all at risk. Even the slightly curious.

"Control follows," she continues. "The high makes you feel you're in control, even though that sounds, erm—"

"Contradictory?"

"That's it. The high makes you feel you're in control, even though that sounds contradictory. I know it looks like people using drugs appear to others as if they're out of control, but I'm telling you, that's not how it feels."

"That's a powerful statement, because I think that when people see ... okay, when *I* saw someone in a state of what we call strung out or high ... that the last thing that person would be feeling is control. So, basically, we're looking at people we think are not in control, and they may not be at all in control ... but inside themselves they feel like they are in control?"

"Total control." She must have noticed the confusion on my face, because she continues. "I know it doesn't look that way. I know it makes no sense. But it's the truth. I felt like I was in control when under the influence of my drugs."

"This is new information to me."

"I didn't realize at the time that I was, what do you call it, self medicating? I did have some internal turmoil. Maybe it was the constant pressure to be all I could be."

"But you were curious, you experimented, and then using made you feel in control ..." I think I understand now. "So you did it again, and again, until you were unable to stop. There probably was a lot of pressure on you as an extreme athlete and high performer in academics. Even though all those skills came naturally to you—there was something inside that just clicked for you when you were curious and tried using drugs."

"I told you, when I tried, out of curiosity, I felt in control. I know you don't want to hear that it felt good for me, but it did."

"No, I'm trying to understand. I need to hear what it was like for you. Your truth." I take a deep breath, let it out slowly. "Of course, you're right, I don't want to hear it was some amazing experience for you. But if it's that way for you and others, then I can see how hard it would be to walk away from."

"As I got into the harder stuff, I knew I wanted to stop but I couldn't. I found myself turning into someone I didn't want to be, but giving up the high wasn't worth getting myself back. Or so I thought. With addiction, you don't realize you're completely losing yourself and losing the relationships around you. The people who care about you most. It just happens."

"How do you make it through each day?"

"Maybe just how everyone else does. Think about the good times. Try to live in the moment. Be grateful. That kind of stuff."

"For me, I know that remembering the little slice of heaven we grew up on is a big part of how I sustain myself."

"It's no different for me. My memory isn't as good as yours, but I know those early years keep me sane at the hardest times."

"That foundation sustains us."

"If you want to say it that way, Toots. But yes."

"Thank you. For answering that question I've had for a long time. One that I buried. And thank you for your honesty. I love you, PK."

"I love you too, Toots."

Chapter 18:
Escalation

It was 1998 and I was sixteen. I found myself feeling proud of my independence—I now had my driver's license and a 1992 Chevy Cavalier, and I was secure with a solid group of friends.

Pam had become much less than her former self, and while I wished she would snap out of being involved with her druggie crowd and her massive mood swings and hateful speech, I knew that realistically, she could not just snap out of it. At Mom's, I'd still find various drugs scattered around, with no idea of what most of them were. When Pam was home, she still holed up in her room—our room—until after supper. When she'd emerge, I'd need to read her facial expressions to know if it was safe to talk to her.

One day, I'd driven to Mom's, and I decided to ask Pam about some things that had gone missing from our bedroom. I went into the kitchen and started simply, without accusation. "Hey, have you seen my curling iron?"

The air was sucked out of the room as she flew into a rage, rising up from the sofa and making her body twice the size of its now customary slumped position. Profanities were hurled at me and around me and were deafening. The anger that contorted her face was all the proof I needed to confirm that she had stolen it.

I rose past my six-feet height. "If you touch my things again, those will be the last things you touch," I warned her.

She stared me down and took a forceful step towards the counter, full Hulk mode.

There was a glint from her right hand. I did a double take. She was gripping the handle of a large, serrated kitchen knife.

In less than a few seconds, she had me up against the old wood paneling that lined the kitchen wall. It was as if I'd been hit by a truck. As I caught my breath, she placed the knife's blade against my neck. She delivered a growling, "How dare you accuse me!"

The flat side of the cold blade pressed against my pulsing vein. She pushed it against my skin, using just enough pressure to avoid drawing blood—something I surmised because I did not see any blood spray out, nor did I feel any warmth around the blade.

She stretched up as close as she could to my face, then spit another statement at me, keeping the knife at my throat. Her words were impossible to discern because her anger turned them into no more than a stunted series of sounds.

There was a strange calm beneath the storm that had been brewing in me. I was sick of it. She had ruined everything. A kinder me—a past me—would have wanted to break down and beg the creature in front of me to bring Pam back. I would remind myself that this monster in front of me was *not* Pam. But I was not wearing my rose-colored glasses now. A fuse attached to the anger that had been building in me. It began to spark and then sizzle. Any memories of heaven on fifteen acres, basketball nights, sodas after softball were now gone.

The blade jiggled at my neck—pressure in an uneven, bumpy line from the knife's serrations.

I'd had enough. As equally as drugs had possessed her, rage and retribution fueled my will to live and took over me. The hurt from her betrayals surged in me and pushed fear well into the background.

A mammoth strength seized my entire body, and in one smooth motion, I grabbed the knife and threw it to the floor. "Don't you ever threaten me again," I snarled.

We advanced hand-to-hand in a dance of anger that took us into the living room of Mom's little house. Then, with more strength than I ever knew I could possess, I suddenly pushed Pam so hard that I became a cannon launching her with so much force her feet were lifted from the ground and she became a projectile. In one movement, her heavy airborne body shattered through the living room picture window.

It played out as if in an action movie. But we were not being filmed, nor were we body doubles for someone else. We were human beings who had been born as sisters and who were now at best strangers to each other—and, in this moment, perhaps even enemies. She'd held a knife to my throat. I'd propelled her through a wide pane of glass.

Shards of glass littered the floor like confetti. I could see there were more outside than inside, as the thin pane had basically traveled with her, in front of her body.

Pam lay on the front lawn, completely still. I stood staring at her from inside the home, through the glass confetti, taking the time for my breath to help slow my heartbeat. She could have killed me. I could have killed her. She lay still except for her rising chest.

The sticky heat of the evening floated in from the gash where the window had been, the song of the cicadas following in a relentless, electric tune. I poked my way over between pieces of broken glass. I walked out the front door—still avoiding broken pieces outside—stepped past her prone body, and got into my little neon-blue Cavalier to drive off. The back of my legs stuck to the seat—the adrenaline-fueled sweat of a midsummer night's fight.

I gripped the steering wheel and stared straight ahead, wishing the act of driving could somehow transport me back to the days when we were inseparable. The tires crunched on the gravel on the driveway as I sped off. I glanced in the rearview. She was still lying in the front yard.

The incident was never discussed.

Chapter 19:
Pam Starts to Open

I was 17. It was sometime in 1999. Incidents with Pam had become almost normalized, and I'd long stopped thinking I'd remember this day or that day as either some turning point or a worst point.

I was just coming into the house at Dad's after swim practice. The phone was ringing and I ran to pick it up.

"Honey, I need you to pray for your sister. She's been in an accident of some sort." Mom was barely able to speak. "I don't know all the details yet, but I got a call from a woman in North Carolina. Pam was found nearly lifeless in a ditch."

I stood listening to my heartbeat.

"Did you hear me, honey?" asked Mom.

"Yes," I responded.

"Sorry to call you with awful news. I'll call back as soon as I hear more—but for now, your sister obviously needs our prayers."

Later that evening, we learned that a kind woman had stopped when she'd seen Pam's body in the ditch.

Pam had been raped and beaten by a drug dealer that she'd connected with during her time in North Carolina. Heath was stationed in Camp Lejeune in Jacksonville, near the mid coastal section of North Carolina, but was deployed at that time. Pam had made her way to the state to visit with his wife.

After this incident, we largely parted ways for the next ten years of her addiction. I heard from Pam every few months and learned to tell from her voice when she was using and when she was not. Time passed. The close relationship I once held with her was lost to the addiction and concurrent lifestyle that accompanied her everywhere she went. Over time, my attitude towards her gradually changed. My knowledge of the science of addiction improved, making me want to understand why she wasn't Pam anymore. I wanted to understand her now more than I wanted to judge her.

❧

"You were far away," Pam's voice brings me back. "Just now."

"I was thinking about Genesis 50:20. What the enemy meant for evil, God worked and turned and intended for good … so that I could preserve and save many lives and people."

"I've heard that before. But I've not been reading the Bible. There are a lot of pages. I can't focus that way." She pauses. "Not like when I was that A student."

"If you're not comfortable talking about those years, I completely respect that. There was a bit of silence a moment ago and I want to make sure you're okay with this."

"I do want to tell you about it, so maybe it can help others. But you know I don't always remember what words to say." Again, a slight pause before she says with determination, "But I want to tell it all. To help others."

"That's amazing. You're amazing. I don't tell you that often enough." I lean forward in my chair. "You really are amazing, and if I could personally rewind all these years and go back to our high school days, I'd do it in a heartbeat—for you." As I lean back again, I say, "I think the stuff we say or do that we think might be bad or wrong—you know, the hard stuff in our lives—even if self-inflicted, well, I think God will use it for good. People don't set out in life to go down the wrong path, but when they do—and there are many times I have myself—their pain becomes a way to help them grow, and to help others as well. So, as you tell me your story, know it can be that bright guiding light that impacts others."

We both use the window again as a pause button. The sun streams through as if giving permission to begin.

"Thanks, Toots. I'm ready to tell my story. Don't know where to start."

"How about when you got out of high school?"

"Do you remember when they found me raped and beaten in the ditch in North Carolina, when I went out to see Heath and Jenny?"

"I'm really sorry you went through that."

"I know you are." She continues, her voice a near whisper. "I was already using, and when I went out to North Carolina—I was headed to where he was stationed but I didn't get that far; I don't remember how close I got. Along the way, I met other people who were dealers and users. I didn't really have much money on me, so when I used their drugs and couldn't pay, they did that to me. They beat me, raped me, beat me while raping me because I didn't have the money. I can't tell you what I was wearing, or what town I was near. I was in a ditch. I was nothing."

We take a window pause.

"Heath was serving overseas when that happened, so Jenny came to the hospital to be with me. You'd think I could have just settled then, with such a good person helping me. Why I didn't stay somewhere safe, like she offered, I don't know. I guess the drugs didn't want me to stay there. I don't know how I always found people who were into drugs, but I did."

"You weren't you when you were addicted. Maybe desperate people find each other. Maybe there's some kind of sixth sense around it."

"Yeah, that's a smart thing to say. It really isn't hard to find people who are on drugs or who can get you drugs. It's pretty easy, actually."

I wish it weren't. "I wish it weren't, for all the people in the world who are addicted."

"There you go. Wishing." She looks directly at me. "The reality is, it's a tough world, Toots. Thank God for root beer and chips."

"We haven't even had any root beer yet today."

"There are chips too."

"I saw that. Keep me away from them or the next thing we'll be streaming *Dirty Dancing* and *Shag*, and I'll be sleeping over."

It's good to see PK laugh. I wait for the right moment to resume our chat.

"I do wish a lot, but I also do the kind of wishing to make things happen. Like fighting for your rights and those of others." *Is this coming out the right way?* "I'm not trying to sound condescending; I'm just saying that wishing or daydreaming can turn to more when it's followed by action."

Chapter 20:
My Dancing Mother

"Tricia, do you think it looks nicer parted on this side?" Mom pushed her curls around.

I was still sometimes measuring time by where Pam was and wasn't. It must have been 1999, because Pam left the year before. I spent time at both parents', but at this point, I was living with Mom.

I sat, fully dressed, in the empty bathtub of the single bathroom Mom and I shared, my long legs taking up its entire length. This was a common resting place for girl talk while Mom got herself ready to go either to work or out dancing.

Four cats, Mom, and I were the residents of this two-bedroom duplex that I loved.

I sat admiring Mom as she curled her hair. Paul Mitchell hairspray, used in abundance to ensure her perfect curls did not budge, floated around us. Michael Bolton's "How Can We Be Lovers" drifted in from the living room, playing on repeat on the CD player we shared.

Mom was a mega babe and Michael Bolton was her heartthrob, and his music played exclusively when she was home. After the divorce, she'd remained a loving and caring mother and also began to explore her own independence.

Fun loving, work-hard-play-hard: These terms perfectly described our dancing-queen mother. After the divorce and before we lost Pam, when Mom wasn't taking us to Cactus Moon on Sunday nights for the family line-dancing extravaganza—which we enjoyed with our friends and their mothers—she was busting a move at one of Kansas City's nightclubs. She also loved to shop. Boy, did she love to shop! And she befriended everyone she met—no one a stranger! A carefree and independent spirit, just like her own mother had been. My tomboyishness contrasted strikingly with her beauty and her beauty regimen.

It wasn't until later, after I'd experienced a lot more of life, and almost as much time in therapy as life, that I realized how Mom's wilder choices after the divorce stemmed from shame—a shame which was rooted in the judgment of others.

When Mom was at her best, she was more fun than engaged—she had flare, she danced, she was fully present with the entire family at big gatherings. Sometimes, more a friend than a mother. Parenting styles were more liberal in the 1980s, and Mom had that wild and exotic Maltese in her. She never quite fit into the quiet small-town life that she tried to embrace.

Chapter 21:
Leaving Home

My senior year of high school—year 2000—was epic. My friends were amazing and my desire to enter adulthood was unbridled. I was crowned prom queen. I probably got the most votes because I was nice to everyone—I learned that from my mom. I was still a tomboy through and through, and hadn't reached the age yet where I was comfortable wearing a dress.

I was totally unprepared when they announced the results of the voting. When they did, I was looking at my bestie, Nicole, convinced she would win. I wanted to be the first to congratulate her.

As they called my name, I let out a giggle and didn't even stand up to go receive my prize of the prom queen crown. To me, claiming the headpiece was just a formality. Had it been a state championship trophy for athletics, I would have been out of my seat with great enthusiasm.

It got better—as in more ridiculous. Because of my height, no store-bought prom dress fitted me properly, so a seamstress was necessary. I had one request: that the dress touch the floor like all the other girls' dresses did. The fabric chosen was a transparent seafoam green.

The pictures showed me on that dance floor, floating in a sea of green, my undergarments shining brightly like diamonds, for everyone in junior and senior class to take in as the King and Queen danced the honorary dance. I'm probably the only prom queen whose panties got more attention than the person wearing them.

Why the seamstress didn't line it, I don't know—nor did anyone else point out the problem prior to the event.

After graduation, I started my freshman year at Southwest Baptist University with the goal of becoming a teacher. I deeply wanted to become a stay-at-home mom or have the flexibility of being available for the children I'd have in the future.

After a few financial aid hiccups, I faced the reality that I couldn't afford the tuition on my own. I transferred to community college in Longview to obtain my associate's degree. After receiving it, I transferred again—to the University of Central Missouri to finish my bachelor's degree in Business Administration. A college professor had talked me out of a teaching degree and into business. One reason was the concern I had over my ability to deal with parents who mistreat their children—anger welled up inside me whenever I encountered child mistreatment. I was not sure how I'd handle it other than be personally unable to let it go. If I switched to business, I could advocate in different ways and from a wider scope.

I met Tony during my sophomore year of college. We lived in the same community and kept bumping into each other. He had a beautiful daughter named Kailey who was six years old when we met. Tony and I connected on two important levels: We had church in common, and we both loved children.

We married in 2004. I was twenty-two years old and still in my undergraduate program. I was so excited for the future and my role of becoming a mother. Three months after we married, I learned I was pregnant with a daughter. My life was falling into place. I had fallen madly in love with Kailey, and now had my own baby on the way.

The satisfying marriage I had pictured was unfolding: I wanted a perfect home filled with love and ease, with babies cooing from cradles; toddlers napping peacefully around me, their stay-at-home mom; the children growing into learners who would be homeschooled with Jesus at the center of their education.

Grace Elizabeth Louise was born on July 7, 2005. She had the most beautiful head of blonde peach fuzz, which quickly landed her the nickname Peach. She decided to come into the world a month early, but I didn't mind that one bit. I got to avoid the brutal last month of pregnancy in the heat of summer. I had to remind myself constantly how much I loved summer that year.

I was smitten with my girls. I had always prayed that my Grandma Barbarick would get to meet my children, and that prayer indeed came true. Grandma was just as lovestruck with Grace as I was!

Four months after Grace was born, Grandma Barbarick fell and broke her leg. Shortly after, pneumonia sadly set in. Grandma Barbarick passed on December 17th. My soul was ripped out of me. I was not prepared for the hard loss. Grandma was the person I had cherished the most. Despite my grieving, Grace and Kailey brought me much happiness. After Grandma left us, life seemed to only get harder and more complicated. There were so many times I sure could have used her wisdom and listening ear.

Pam was not in the picture at all. She'd come and go with little fanfare. I remained hopeful—or rather, prayerful—that there might be a huge change for the positive in her life. Beyond sending prayers, however, I was not in any position to help her.

Chapter 22:
White Picket Fences

Somewhere on the road to *happily ever after*, there was a major detour and life presented me with its own plan. Sometime between Tony getting hurt on the job, his own unhealed childhood trauma, and my unhealed wounds from my parents' divorce and subsequently losing the Pam that I once knew, we both dove headfirst into an unhealthy relationship.

The marriage became marked by cycles of highs and lows. This situation looked like handling the frustration of someone who was in constant pain and who wanted to go back to work—but whose injury prevented that. It looked like me trying to say and do everything right so that the proverbial white picket fences magically just appeared for Tony and me. Him raging, and me walking on eggshells.

My heart often went out to Tony, completely. However, as I was tasked to care for him more, there was subsequently little of my own heart or energy left for me. I often felt like a boat tossing in a storm.

There were moments of calm. The girls especially were my place of peace and joy. But I was a wife without clear boundaries. I lacked assertiveness. I had no idea I was opening the door to behaviors that eroded my self-worth and emotional well-being. While I believe that God, love, and trust are meant to be the foundation of a marriage, the absence of boundaries distorted those ideals into a rigid denial of truth.

In short order, unhealthy patterns—including my lifelong people pleasing—began to first resurface and then take root. In the absence of boundaries, tolerance flourished. I learned to tolerate everything. I found myself shrinking, losing sight of the bold, young woman I had been in college. The once strong and feisty Tricia now feared confrontation and hung tight to the ideologies I had been taught regarding marriage. *Marry once and forever.* I embraced a cycle of denial to protect the illusion of normalcy. I couldn't even think of the word *fail*—so far was I from understanding that life is filled with learning, and that we learn from missteps. I saw an unhealthy and potentially toxic marriage as a misstep. Something that could be course-corrected.

I became profoundly isolated. I started reading to fill the space that my social interactions had once inhabited.

Slowly, I began to learn how boundaries are not just lines drawn in the sand; they are declarations of self-worth and the framework for fruitful relationships. Once I began reclaiming boundaries, I rediscovered some of my self-worth, and I found myself embarking on a transformative journey.

Starting that journey empowered me to find courage and boldness—to harness the confidence I had shared with my sister and friends in sports, and bring it to the rest of my life. I began to see that being assertive does not mean being combative; it means honoring intrinsic values and refusing to accept anything less than respectful treatment. I also started on the path to understanding that my worth is not determined by what I endured, but rather by the courage I find to reclaim myself.

Of course, experience and knowledge is great in hindsight. While I was in the dark places within my marriage, I repeated the dysfunctional behaviors, slowly losing pieces of who I was, bending and reshaping myself to keep the waters still.

Put simply, the dynamics within our marriage did not allow a soft place to fall or provide the safety net that marriage should offer. Instead, I traveled further away from who I was at my core. I was left confused and hurt.

A desire for forgiveness and healing, a consideration for the peace of mind of our beautiful girls, and a deep respect for Tony's and my dignity all negate any reason to detail the darkness and hurt that transformed the center of our marriage.

There came a time where the marriage was no longer sustainable to me. I did what was best for myself and my girls. I ended it. We divorced in 2007.

Kailey was a huge part of my life, despite not being my biological daughter. We worked out that she would spend a weekend a month with me. From my warrior-mother's point of view, those times were so precious to me.

A flame ignited within me that fueled me to work ferociously to provide for my girls. This led to my desire to become fiercely independent. Not only did I work to be attuned to the needs of my own girls, but I now also became an advocate for other girls. This is not to imply that life was all applesauce and rainbows: The beauty that was revealed and the new authentic life that was unfolding before us meant that I also shouldered a tremendous amount of shame at my perceived failure to be that white-picket-fence wife. I was young and inexperienced. I had so much growing up to do; I just did not realize that at the time. I thought I should know it all in my twenties. But none of us know it all at any age. Least of all in our twenties.

Chapter 23:
The Journey
to Transformation

The year after the divorce, I purchased a house for me and the girls. I was hugely proud of this accomplishment. The year after that, 2009, I decided to advance in my career in finance. Even though I said I'd never step foot into another classroom again, I decided to go for my master's degree. I did it for my girls. I felt a master's degree in finance would be a great start for a single mom who had no plans of ever marrying again.

Tony and I shared joint custody of Grace, with Grace spending every other weekend with Tony. I also still had Kailey once a month. Our routine was beautiful and peaceful. As a mother and daughters, we thrived. Tuesday nights I'd bake. Many evenings, I would tuck Grace into her stroller and run, then stop by Poppy's Ice Cream during the summer. We'd read books and play hide-and-seek with her stuffed animals. She'd fall asleep in my arms. We'd garden together. It was lovely. Just the two of us—and three of us when Kailey was here.

Over time, I learned that if the wounds inside us are not healed properly, they fester. Those open wounds often translate to lashing out at others in misdirected frustration. Tony and I had attempted the impossible: to form a healthy marriage of two broken people who did not have the pieces to be fully themselves.

I've noticed that people who hurt others are often fighting their own demons. I believe that most people are filled with goodness; it is just that sometimes, their core is clouded by the pain and hurt they experienced in their own childhood or early adulthood. I know that Tony had wounds that were not healed at the time we married, and I had wounds that were never healed when I said "I do."

When people go on their own healing journey, as both Tony and I decided separately to do, it is possible to meet at a place of support and happiness. Tony and I each worked to heal our wounds and traumas by independently attending counseling and self-discovery in the years after our divorce. We both grew closer to the Divine and to each other in our love walk with Jesus. For me, there is no greater healer.

If I'd been asked in 2007 if Tony and I could one day have the healthy, kind, supportive co-parenting relationship we now do, I would have said that would be impossible.

❧

Transformation doesn't happen overnight. I found myself traveling the path of change for years, one mile at a time, one relationship at a time, one conversation at a time. Such a long journey, with so many complex moving parts and many side trips. Detours, excursions, landmarks, destinations, road break-downs …

One of the most valuable things I've learned, so far, about the journey is that we don't have to travel it alone. Once I understood that life is about building experiences and learning from them, I created a support system that I could access at any time during my life trip. I leaned on my big family, who championed me the whole way. I leaned primarily on my family because for so long, I struggled to ask for help from friends. I was convinced that carrying my pain alone was the only way to protect the people close to me. I pushed friends away, thinking I was shielding them from the weight of my world, when in reality, I was only isolating myself further. What I thought was strength was actually fear disguised as self-preservation. Little did I know that I didn't need to push them away; I needed to pull them closer. I focused most of my energy on building my relationship with my daughters, always seeking to both be a role model for them and to provide them with a stable foundation—no matter what was going on with me.

I held space for the pain of the past, I started to enjoy the gift of the present, and I looked forward to a future built from healing.

It took a long time to dissect the different parts of myself so that I could find a balance, so that I could genuinely care for and about others rather than people-please, and put myself first. It took a while to love myself unconditionally.

Even with amazing things happening, including working hard, achieving success, celebrating and participating in the girls' lives, and loving being a mother, a part of my journey includes a number of important years that I came to call *wandering in the wilderness*, during which my faith went dormant. It never left me. I would still pray and always felt a pull to lean back on my faith, but I went through a drought. The enemy of life had convinced me that life as a Christian was too hard. He convinced me that a woman so broken could not serve God. It took me years to realize that God and my faith were the only steady presence in my life. Instead of turning away, I should have turned to Him. Life would have been far more peaceful and purposeful during those years. Life was still a sweet symphony and from the outside looking in; I appeared to have so much of my life together. The truth was, I began to wither on the inside, dried out by the weight of the world, because I believe our souls were not meant to survive without God, our Living Water.

Chapter 24:
Ambitions

As I discovered the grueling schedule that comes with starting a master's degree, I simultaneously discovered coffee. It started as a love–hate relationship, but we worked through it. I knew I could not get through all of those sleepless nights without it. Between staying up until two in the morning studying, and Grace's stage of going through night terrors, I was not getting much sleep. I was fueled by passion, love, and coffee. I learned to love everything about it—from its roasted aroma to its deep, rich taste.

In the fall of 2009, friends said they wanted to set me up with another friend of theirs. I had zero interest in dating or ever remarrying. I refused multiple requests, but I eventually said yes to a date.

Dale and I became fast friends. He was the kind of person who could make anyone laugh and put people quickly at ease. His quick wit and a natural sense of humor was a welcoming presence. He knew how to lighten even the heaviest moment. His warm and inviting presence was just what I needed.

I started helping him often with his daughter Reagan, of whom he had full custody. Dale traveled in his work, and since

I loved children—all children—I wanted to help him. I helped care for Reagan when my schedule allowed.

Reagan was six years old: two years older than Grace. Kailey was twelve. Dale and I gave dating a go, but the chemistry or something in me didn't feel right, so I called it off. I was too comfortable with the life I had, and was scared to jump back into a serious physical and emotional relationship.

Even though my primary focus remained on my girls and business, I continued to explore my interest in children and in the relationships between children and their caregivers. While working and obtaining my master's degree online from Stephens College, I also got the bright idea to become licensed in the state of Missouri for assisting families and individuals with adoptions.

I was sick of hearing about the outrageous cost of adoption. It pushes adoption out of reach for many loving people, and I determined that I would find a way around that barrier. Instead of opening an adoption agency, I obtained my license in order to be a liaison for those interested in adoption, thus able to cut out much of the cost that agencies charged. I wanted to connect families directly with the attorneys and social workers needed to finalize adoptions at a more affordable cost. I wanted to assist families in obtaining the adoption credit the state of Missouri offered families who adopt. I was beyond merely fulfilled at a job with this work. I had discovered my purpose in life, and I was thriving. My career in finance paid the bills; my side work in adoption fed my soul and pushed me to go further.

In the spring of 2010, when Grace was five years old, I decided to apply to law school. My desire to advocate for underprivileged children was gnawing at me. I now felt that having a law degree would broaden my credibility to speak up for those who cannot speak for themselves. I took the LSAT and was accepted into the University of Missouri–Kansas City law program for the following fall.

I celebrated my acceptance into law school by booking a trip to the island of Malta to meet the rest of my mother's large family. I couldn't wait to tell our distinguished Uncle Maurice that I would follow in his footsteps in law—and though he had used his degree as a diplomat, serving as Ambassador for sixteen countries, mine would be used to fight for the rights for children.

The other thing I did was pray. I prayed especially for Pam, as she was always on my mind. She was struggling so much, and there still wasn't a thing I could do for her, other than pray. The few times she got in touch, I also let her know I could be there for her if she wanted me to be, or if she once again needed me to beat up a bully. What I did not fully realize until much later was just how strong Pam was—how she had defied the laws of survival in every way possible. On her journey, alongside bipolar disorder, she had physical health issues that included infections and untreated wounds, concurrent with the life-threatening effects of overdoses. Many of her body systems suffered irreparable damage.

We were both resilient in different ways. Pam fought through homelessness, violence, and dangerous medical emergencies caused by the various combinations of drugs she put into her system. She was a natural-born fighter. I was navigating shame and guilt, people-pleasing, and suppressed emotions because my personality is one of a servant and an optimist. I never stopped or slowed. I pushed myself forward. I did this perhaps to make up for Pam's loss of her own passion. I became more present in my own life to make up for her absence in hers.

Chapter 25:
Malta

Before I was slated to enter law school and start that new grueling schedule, I traveled to Malta to visit the extended family that I'd heard so much about. I had met only a handful of my aunts and an uncle, but I was anxious to meet the rest of my Maltese family.

The charming island of Malta was even more beautiful and vibrant than I had expected: I'd never seen such a vivid blue sea, and the stones with which many buildings were constructed took me back centuries. Its many fortresses and cathedrals are a structural echo of the Italian and Spanish rulers who had lived on the island, and its vineyards made my mouth water, anticipating the full-bodied wine I'd be served. Some of the roads were still beaten and broken from the island being hit by numerous bombs during World War II. The 7,000-year-old ruins on the island and the short ferry ride to Gozo were beautiful. The Azure Window in Gozo was incredible. Sadly, it would collapse a few years later, in 2017.

Incredible as the sights were, it was my legendary family who captured the majority of my attention. Eating that first meal together at Aunt Vicki's, surrounded by joyful people and food that had been so lovingly prepared—I really felt like I was home.

The table was covered in every imaginable Maltese dish, from timpana—baked pasta—to a dessert called prinjolata, which is part biscuit and sponge cake covered with frosting, glacé cherries, and chocolate.

Every member of the family showed an interest in one another's activities, asking about their day, prompting them to expand on simple experiences they'd had on the way there. Between the stories, each person took the time to taste their food and share how they felt about the flavors.

This family was everything and more. Aunt Terry—a leading actress in Malta for three decades—told stories that had us crying in laughter. It was exhilarating. I had never laughed so hard! It was difficult to discern which we partook more of: eating or laughing. We shared hilarious stories about Grandma Hammons—I even learned on that trip that when Grandpa Hammons met her, she was already engaged to a future President of Malta.

It was slated to be the wedding of the century, according to my great-uncle Maurice. The uniting of two diplomatic families was the talk of the island. Madeline Teresa Carman Pia Ore Lubrano came from an affluent family of diplomats, and if she married the man she was engaged to, she would become First Lady of Malta one day. But the devilishly handsome soldier from America found his way into the heart of my royally engaged grandmother.

He swept my grandmother off her feet and carried her away to America. Well, kind of.

When Madeline called off the wedding of the century, her parents were so disapproving, they forced her to leave the island. She went to London, pregnant with twins, and stayed there until it was time to deliver. One of those twins was my mom.

Mom and her twin sister, our Aunt Sassy Bubble-gum, were born in St. Mary's Hospital in Paddington. Grandpa returned to America to save money and obtain visas for his fiancée and the twins to come to America. It took a great deal of time, but eventually he made his way back to his sweetheart, then brought his family home. Then Grandma and Grandpa had four more children.

No wonder Grandma was so bold, wild, and confident. She'd had the world at her feet. The red lipstick and glamour began to make sense.

The trip continued. Uncle Maurice took me from Sliema to visit Valletta, and on to Mdina. He took me touring everywhere, and we had unlimited access to places, since Uncle Maurice and Aunt Terry were treated like royalty in Malta. Store owners wouldn't even let me pay for the items I wanted to buy to bring back home.

We visited the magnificent St. John's Co-Cathedral in Valletta, dedicated to John the Baptist. Its most striking feature, and the one that intrigued me the most, was the floor. Covered with inlaid polychrome marble in a myriad of colors, the floor is comprised of images of the people buried in the more than 400 tombstones that it covers. They are the tombs of some of the most influential individuals in history, including Knights of the Order. The cathedral is also home to Caravaggio's original painting, *The Beheading of Saint John the Baptist*, which was completed in 1608 in Malta. It was very moving to behold in person. My uncle also took me to what is considered the location of Paul's shipwreck, which was mentioned in the Bible, and the Church of St. Paul on the site where Paul worshipped while he was stranded on Malta. A fantastically spiritual experience, indeed.

While I was in Malta, I drank more cappuccino than I had ever dreamed of drinking, which was heaven on earth! I ate the famous pastizz, which is a pastry filled with ricotta and seasonings. *Kemm hu tajjeb*—delicious!

That too-short week filled my soul with the healing that comes from meeting family who were beyond generous and beautiful. For the first time in a long while, though Pam was in my prayers, I got a break from the huge responsibility surrounding her that I had shouldered, including a reprieve from answering questions about her. In Malta, the relatives did not know about Pam's situation, nor did I speak of it. Of course, I wished we could have been there together and that there had never been any addiction, but that was a wish. I let myself indulge and be indulged.

Part Three:
Allie's Story

Chapter 26:
Sugar Bear

I returned from Malta, ready to start law school. I had my girls, I was reflecting on my future with Dale, and I had renewed faith that I was blessed. If only I could find a way to include Pam— the Pam I once knew—and be part of the light that could help her heal.

Five-year-old Grace was my sweet sugar bear. We had a beautiful routine that included putting on music and dancing the second we came home to the house, then cooking together. We'd settle down by painting fingernails and cuddling until we fell asleep. We had single mother–daughter-together life down to an art.

There was nothing Grace wanted for that I could not give her, except a baby sister. She'd often told me she wanted to be a big sister. She wanted a sibling so badly, it became part of many conversations.

I spent the summer months working and soaking up the girls. Work was amazing and I couldn't wait for the future. Dale, the girls, and I began spending a lot more time together. Sometime that summer, we decided to give dating another go. He then became a steadier presence in my life. He was funny and hardworking, and an incredible father, raising Reagan all on his own. After we started by going on a few dates, Dale began talking about marriage, since he wanted Reagan to have a stable mother figure. He also thought I should have one more layer to my support system—that layer being him. He tried convincing me with the logic that, because we were best friends, got along so well, and because we'd both said we'd never remarry, we could thus only marry each other.

I didn't think his proposal was that ridiculous. We loved each other and each other's children. We were both independent. We knew each other. Being best friends was pretty amazing, and Dale was such a stable presence in my life. He certainly planted an idea.

Chapter 27:
Premonitions

Children are my passion. Vulnerable little humans. I had not known exactly how my passion for them would impact my life, but a sense of peace had always washed over me whenever I thought or spoke of adoption.

For years, it had been at the forefront of my mind to adopt a child from another country. I had researched international orphanages in high school; some of the conditions of those orphanages brought me to tears and ignited in me an unquench-able desire to speak up for all the children who could not speak for themselves.

Early in my research, I began praying for God to bless me with a child through adoption and, every time I prayed, I envisioned the same child with—to a rural Midwesterner—exotic looks: dark hair, dark eyes, and olive skin. This was often the appear-ance of the children I encountered in photos during my inter-national adoption research, so at first, I did not think anything of it. Then the vision started becoming more recurrent, always the same face.

Adoption. A girl. Dark hair. Dark eyes. Olive skin. She was in my dreams.

This child became a part of a future I somehow, deep inside, knew to be real.

Suddenly, a whirlwind reappeared. Pam came back into our lives and cranked up the energy-love-confusion-frustration-forgiveness temperature dial on the furnace of our family dynamics.

She moved in with Dad, but yet again, disappeared for extended periods of time. After one such disappearance, she returned quietly.

It was June 2010. Dad phoned and told me that Pam had been sick for several weeks. He didn't know what to do. As he began describing her symptoms, I knew it wasn't just an illness. It was morning sickness.

I paused for a moment and quietly whispered in my phone, as though a whisper could minimize the impact of the truth I was about to speak. "Dad, it sounds like Pam is pregnant."

"No, no." Dad was insistent. He argued with me because, previously, a doctor had told us that Pam couldn't get pregnant because of her myriad health issues. I listened to him try to convince himself she couldn't be carrying, and when he finished, I told him to be prepared for that possibility. Doctors can be—and often are—wrong.

I urged Dad to take Pam for a pregnancy test.

A few hours later, he called to say he had taken her to the hospital emergency room. His initial silence was followed by his cracked and devastated voice. It was enough for me to know.

Pam was indeed pregnant.

The devastation Dad—and Mom too—suddenly felt was for good reason: After her now twelve years of bipolar disorder combined with extensive drug abuse, we knew that Pam could neither physically nor emotionally take care of her baby.

I knew in that moment that God wanted me to adopt Pam's baby. I couldn't explain it, but it was as though God had already been preparing my heart.

I saw her again: Dark hair. Dark eyes. Olive skin.

Dad had no idea what was probably going to happen, but I did. And I knew how it would happen. I'd wait for Pam to realize it on her own, too—that is, if she did not already.

The next month, Pam called me and told me she wanted to talk.

I sat in a red booth tucked in the back of Pam's favorite fast food restaurant, Long John Silver's, fidgeting, sipping on a root beer, waiting. Pam and my parents entered and quietly slid into the booth with me. I made eye contact with Pam and saw a peace in her eyes that I had not seen in twelve years. We sat silently for what felt like a long time. No words were spoken until Pam began. I was still processing that peace when Pam broke the silence, abruptly and practically. "Sis, will you adopt my baby?"

I'd known since Dad's phone call, before he'd even taken her to the hospital.

"Yes," I replied. No hesitation. And, oh, how that peace flowed between us. It was infused with light. The light I'd prayed for.

That light encompassed our parents as they sighed in relief. We were enveloped by peace in that moment. All the uncertainty dissipated. We sat quietly, staring at one another, in awe of the gift of life. There was a flutter of unspoken concern: whether the baby might be affected by Pam's drug use.

I broke the silence, letting Pam know that I would love her baby unconditionally, and provide the life that Pam wanted for that child.

For twelve years, I'd watched Pam's hazel eyes dim throughout her struggle. Suddenly, the color returned. I'd missed the vibrancy.

"Yes," said God—or least, I imagined God saying. "There are blessings ahead that none of you can imagine."

Pam made a selfless, courageous decision for the future that day. That of her soon-to-be-born baby, and for herself.

Who knows what profound conversations and decisions happen in everyday fast-food places where people meet for soda and snacks? That summer of 2010, in a red booth at Long John Silver's, a single conversation verified the statement, *Whenever two or more gather in His name, He is present.*

I came home and started making my own preparations. Including the tough decision to rescind my acceptance into law school. There was no way I could juggle the adoption process and caring for an infant while meeting the demands of a grueling academic program. I did not tell Pam, as I did not want her to feel guilty over my decision.

Chapter 28:
Pregnancy

Pam asked me to accompany her to her first doctor's appointment. The week before we went, she insisted that she knew who the father was. She told me he was a white truck driver and that he would want nothing to do with having a baby, so I would not have to worry about him signing over his rights. I had already contacted a lawyer to discuss the legal aspects of the adoption and, in that initial meeting, he told me he could assist with the paperwork needed for the birthfather to sign over to me.

When I picked Pam up at Dad's, exhaustion was etched into her face. I understood how pregnancy itself can be exhausting, and she'd also had a nasty stretch of morning sickness. On top of that, her health hadn't been great when she'd become pregnant. She was still wearing mismatched clothes that reflected a complete disarray in her life rather than an eclectic taste. Her shoulder-length hair hadn't been thoroughly brushed. I thought to myself how it was a reminder for me of the chaos she'd been living. Despite her rough exterior, I sensed vulnerability as she eased herself into the car. Her hand shook when I reached out to squeeze it on the ride to the clinic.

We went into the first appointment anxious to know how far along she was and if her baby was healthy.

The waiting room was more of a hallway and featured hard chairs jammed close together: chairs that offered neither softness nor room to spread out. A 1960s coffee table with out-of-date, much-handled magazines. If we'd volunteered to paint, we might have done structural damage, so thin were the walls. And because of that, there was so much interference—noise from every part of the building. Nothing was private for the patients; therefore, nothing could be sacred, either.

When we arrived, we were taken into a small, off-white office and told to wait a moment for the doctor. It wasn't the kind of warm, welcoming office that I first sat in when I was expecting Grace: that one with the tabletop waterfall in the corner of the well-decorated space. Again, we sat in hard institutional chairs on a scuffed floor in a room that also had not been painted since the day it was built more than forty years before. Even with the door closed, the hustle and bustle of staff tending to women filtered through. Medicaid. Can't live without it. Almost can't live with it.

"I don't know how I'm gonna afford this baby." A woman's voice spoke to another woman whom I assumed was a doctor or nurse. I didn't want to know this person's business. I almost covered my ears and wished for music. I wasn't thinking a complete revamp with speakers, but perhaps a portable CD player in each room could help with boundaries. I looked over at Pam and saw how her eyes were darting around the room, as if searching for a way to escape not only the room but the situation. Her previously bright eyes were shadowed by fear and weariness. At first, she stared expressionless at the dirty walls, then she looked only into her lap. The longer we waited, the smaller she seemed. It was as though the weight of all her choices had started catching up to her.

My heart broke a little as I realized that Pam wasn't going to receive the same level of either care or concern I had received for my pregnancy. Such disparity between the care of women who had health insurance and women who didn't.

My thoughts were interrupted by the door opening. We were met by a doctor whose beige pants and shirt mirrored the efficiency of scrubs. Her posture was ramrod straight, and her feet pushed forward in the kind of hurried step that announced a potential to pivot at a moment's notice. We were meaningless numbers on uncomfortable chairs; she was a busy professional in an overburdened system—the dark circles under her eyes said it all.

She introduced herself to Pam and me, then unleashed a series of questions for Pam. The distinct lack of emotion and the list-like delivery cut into me. I was so distracted by her lack of bedside manner that I heard none of her questions that followed: *1) Confirm name. 2) Is this your birth date? 3) Have you had previous pregnancies?* Not even a *please*. I became lost in what I perceived to be a lack of genuine caring for these women. This doctor seemed annoyed that there was yet another pregnant woman in her care who was struggling in life. I extended my disappointment and anger to the entire staff.

With each abrupt checklist question, Pam's fragility was magnified. It was clear that she was battling demons far bigger than she could handle alone. I reached over and held her hand, letting her know she didn't have to handle anything alone, because I was there.

When I found myself included in the conversation, Pam informed the doctor that I was going to adopt her baby. For a second, the doctor softened. Her eyes were a little brighter; there was a slight change to the straightness of her lips. She set down her pen and reached out to shake my hand. It was disheartening to notice the difference in how she treated me versus how she had been treating Pam. I had no idea regarding the experiences the doctor had been exposed to through her patients. I engaged in the handshake.

I battled internally between wanting to judge and wanting to understand. *She had not shaken Pam's hand.*

At that point, the doctor began speaking at me, not to me, and not with Pam.

I felt myself prickle. Every human deserves to be treated with dignity and respect. I gathered up my energy and said, "Pam is going to be caring for and carrying her baby until she gives birth, so I would really appreciate it if you could treat her with respect and speak to her, not me."

A look of surprise crossed the doctor's face. I might have been the first person ever to speak to her in that manner.

She apologized and addressed Pam with some level of respect. She told us we'd be moving rooms for an ultrasound, and that she'd see us at the follow-up appointment.

We were greeted by an extremely sweet ultrasound tech who spoke to Pam in a loving manner. I could tell she had been informed of Pam's decision. We discovered that Pam was already almost five months along, and that the baby was a girl.

Pam and I shared a smile. After the technician wiped Pam's belly and handed her a series of images, I leaned over, kissed her belly, and whispered, "I can't wait to meet you, little girl. You are going to be so loved."

When we got back to the car after the appointment, I could see a look of concern on Pam's face. I asked her if everything was okay. "I didn't realize I was so far along. Do you think the drugs I've been using have hurt her or are hurting her now? I promised I would quit using while I am pregnant. I don't want her to be affected by the drugs."

I reassured her by leaning on my faith.

"God will take care of our sweet little girl. You just focus on the next few months, one day at a time, okay?"

We talked about the importance of balance during the pregnancy: vitamins, water, stress reduction. Then I contemplated the future in silence. She broke it by blurting out, "I think there may be another potential birthfather."

More silence ensued.

"He's a really good man, but I don't know if he will want custody of her."

I began asking questions about who the new potential birthfather could be. "He's Black. Very good looking. We had a one-night stand. He is one of the nicest guys I had known in a long time."

My heart skipped a beat. *A girl. Dark hair. Dark eyes. Olive skin.*

"Okay." I processed my response. "You need to contact him and inform him, so that we know where this is going to lead."

"I don't know how to get hold of him. This is so embarrassing, Tricia, I called a one-night stand number, and this guy showed up. All I know is where he was working when we hooked up."

A myriad thoughts probably catapulted through my head at that moment; they surely included how she could possibly know he was a really good man if she didn't know how to reach him and had only met him once.

During the rest of Pam's pregnancy, and afterwards, months of emotional turmoil ensued as we tried to locate him: The one-night stand number refused to release any information, and he did not work at the place he'd told Pam. To make things more difficult, the mother of the other potential birthfather had been informed and wanted to take custody and help her son raise his

baby. Pam reminded me that the other guy was completely inca-
pable of taking care of a baby, and begged me to fight them for
custody. This led to more legal fees and more uncertainty, but I
was determined to fight, as Pam had asked, even though we did
not know if he was the birthfather. It became clear when Pam
gave birth that the truck driver was indeed not the birthfather,
and the legal matters were summarily dismissed.

The months after the first doctor's appointment held other
challenges. Pam changed her mind more than once about what
to do. Some family members suggested I was forcing Pam into
adoption. Other family, and some friends, inundated me with
questions: What if the baby was born sick? What if she was
negatively affected by Pam's drug abuse? What if she grew up
with the same mental illness Pam suffered? My answer was and
would always remain, "I will love her all the same."

I never questioned for a moment that God had a huge purpose
for Pam's baby's life. I knew that I was to be her momma.

Pam took absolutely amazing care of herself for the rest of her
pregnancy. It had to have been hard for her to resist, to push
addiction to a corner to ensure she preserved the growing life
within her.

※

Dale of course knew about Pam's situation and my plan to
adopt her child. Throughout the fall, he kept dropping subtle
hints that we should tie the knot. I was still hardened by the
outcome of my first marriage; I truly didn't think I would ever
marry again. That had been my way of protecting myself from
enduring that pain again.

Dale was still my best friend and a phenomenal father to
Reagan. As he kept insisting we were a perfect match, I was

beginning to concede and see that maybe we all needed him in our lives. He argued again how Reagan needed a mom. He knew and loved Grace. He wanted Pam's baby to become ours: She'd have a mom and a dad.

One warm, fall evening after eating Italian and going to the comedy club, Dale dropped to one knee and formally asked me to marry him.

"Yes," I said.

On November 10th, we met during our lunch hour at the Jackson County courthouse for a ceremony. That was Dale and me. Unromantic, practical.

Both of us had focused on our careers and girls and one another. Who needs a big ceremony when you have two low-maintenance people who were ready to start a life together?

Chapter 29:
Allie

All the uncertainties surrounding Pam's pregnancy vanished one cold and snowy Monday: January 17, 2011. I had the pleasure of being in the delivery room with Pam.

A girl. Dark haired. Dark eyes. Olive skin.

She had arrived.

Pam had completed the loving journey she'd agreed to.

Pam had a legacy.

I had a new daughter.

Grace had a baby sister.

God had worked in mysterious ways.

She had a name: Alexandria Kaye-Geneice.

Life ushered in a renewed forgiveness, further purpose, and patience—all delivered to my doorstep in a bundle of baby named Allie.

She was the exact child that I had envisioned since I first daydreamed about adopting. The child with dark hair, dark eyes, and olive skin was on the scale that registered five pounds, fifteen ounces.

For years I had thought that child in my dreams lived in an orphanage in another country—and she was brought to me by my own sister. I became overwhelmed, crying tears of absolute joy.

She was perfection—all babies are. She began her life hearing a loving message from my soul translated as:

"I didn't give you the gift of life, but in my heart I know that the love I feel is deep and real, as if it had been so. For us to have each other is like a dream come true. No, I didn't give you the gift of life; life gave me the life-gift of you."

My thoughts turned again to the Japanese practice of kintsugi—the art of repairing a break or crack in an item with gold, only to then value the object more because now it has a story to become a transformed piece of art, the gold highlighting the scar as part of its evolution.

My soul continued to speak:

"God is a God of restoration. The ultimate kintsugi artist. Addiction may have shattered my relationship with my sister for twelve years, but God repaired our brokenness through the birth of Allie. Allie is both gold and golden."

One of the many Hebrew names of God is Jehovah Rapha: *the God who heals.* In Exodus 15:26, Jehovah heals His people of physical and spiritual ailments. He restores them. He makes them new again.

My soul quoted Psalm 147:3:

He heals the broken in heart,

And binds up their wounds.

I knew with Allie's birth that someday all my sister's wounds would be bound up and she would be given ultimate healing. I wrote in the family Bible:

On January 17, 2011

Amid a winter's snowy blizzard

at 12:59 pm

at the St. Joseph Medical Center in Overland Park,
Kansas

the world changed and became a more beautiful place

Alexandria Kaye-Geneice

was born.

She weighed five pounds fifteen ounces.

Her hair was as soft as the downy feathers of a black
swan

And her bright eyes exotic tones of knowingness

She was absolutely perfect.

Chapter 30: Coming Home

Minutes after Allie was born, I entered the waiting area.

Dad, Mom, and Dale were on the edge of their seats and stood as I approached them.

"She's beautiful," I said. Then I broke down sobbing. My heart told me I was describing both Pam and Allie. My soul told me I was speaking about larger issues of life and love.

Allie came into the world with three big sisters who could not wait to snuggle her. Grace was five, Reagan was seven, and Kailey was fourteen. Dale brought Grace and Reagan to the hospital to meet their little sister. They instantly fell in love. My months of uncertainty slowly dissolved.

The next four days—Allie's first four on this side of the world—were difficult and emotional for me. Pam appeared calm, strong for both of us. Some nurses referred to me as Mom, others to Pam as Mom.

Pam loved Allie with that impossible love that mothers feel when seeing their newborn for the first time. I felt as though I was tearing Allie away from Pam. I didn't leave the hospital; I didn't leave Pam and Allie's side. We were in the midst of a blizzard in Kansas City during our time at the hospital; thus, our visitors were few.

I felt guilty: guilt because Pam went through the pain of delivery and a Caesarian section, and guilt because she wasn't going to get to raise the child she so deeply loved. It was heart-wrenching when the photographer brought in her laptop with the proofs of Allie's first session—the song that was playing was about taking care of your baby and never leaving their side.

I had no appetite and barely slept. These four days felt like four years.

We left the hospital, and I drove Pam to Dad's, where she'd been staying. On the way, I sobbed uncontrollably, to the point that I could hardly see the road. Because Pam chose life for Allie. Because I felt as though Pam didn't fully comprehend the depth of pain ahead: the pain of not getting to see Allie every day, and also still seeing her periodically at family events, on visits, and the like.

At one point I felt selfish for crying, and cried over that, too. That's when Pam looked at me and asked, "Why are you crying? Don't be sad for me; be happy that Allie will have a great life."

I will always admire Pam's strength that day.

I hadn't realized how big Pam's love for Allie was until that moment. Four days after she delivered Allie, had cuddled and kissed her and loved her, I realized suddenly that Pam was stronger and more courageous than I could ever be. The only thing Pam wanted more than to raise her own baby, was for her baby to have the best possible life she could have ... with *me*. And, by extension, our immediate and extended family. Pam was determined that the addiction that had robbed her of a fruitful life would never rob her baby of a beautiful one.

Chapter 31:
Moving

I left Pam at Dad's. I hoped that she would find the strength to remain clean and begin a new chapter for her own life. Allie would benefit from that, as would I. I witnessed some of that hope in action at a baby shower, hosted by our cousin, Jill. Pam had seemed touched by the love and support there. She'd smiled and genuinely been excited by the gifts and the goodwill. I'm definitely not the only one who had clung to the hope that this could be a turning point.

Sadly, Addiction greeted her somewhere between the car and Dad's front door, eager to overrule the motherly passion I knew was in Pam's heart. Addiction, that dark entity, had, like a member of our family, waited for Pam to birth Allie. It now barged back in and resumed its stranglehold on her.

She stayed at Dad's a day or two, then started to drift. She left all her things at his house but began staying away longer. We'd hear a word or two about how she'd been couch-surfing with her friends, then a week or two would go by with no contact. Weeks turned into months. Conversation was sparse and inconstant. There was next to nothing for a good while.

It was a difficult time, filled with unanswered questions and the gnawing worry of not knowing how she was or what she might have been going through. We'd been through it before, but this time it felt different—she'd stayed clean and had her baby and seemed to have wanted to change. All we could do was care for each other now and hope that one day she could find her way back.

The rare times when Pam was in touch, she didn't ask much about Allie. She'd see her at some family gatherings but maintained a distance between them. This was probably her way of protecting her own heart from the heartache of not being able to raise Allie. I told myself it was okay. This was something Pam needed to do.

Maybe, to an extent, guilt and shame played a role in her distance. And awkwardness. Maybe combined shame and PTSD. I would regularly grapple with these are questions.

❧

After bringing Allie into my house, I had two weeks off work. There was no maternity leave for adoption at the company I worked for.

Megan was a massive help with Allie. She took two weeks off work when my two weeks were over. She stayed all day with Allie, and was also there for Grace and Reagan before and after school. Following that, Mom put in two weeks as well. This was a huge comfort to me, and it helped each of us bond with Allie.

Dale and I were granted legal guardianship of Allie for the first six months of her life. This six-month trial period was granted in accordance with Missouri law, which provided a window of time for reunification of child and birthparent or birthparents. Following those first six months, adoption to the legal guardian or guardians could be granted.

During our six months, Dale received a promotion and his company asked him to relocate to Atlanta. I didn't expect this news, and didn't think it would be good for our family dynamic, but in the end, we made the move.

It was a lot to handle. It meant distance from our family and support system. There would be many miles between Grace and her dad. Reagan would need to see her mom. I'd want to still see Kailey, my bonus daughter. It hurt to think I'd be separated from Megan. I'd miss Dad and Mom, too. And what of Allie and Pam seeing each other when Pam was available?

We'd always lived within twenty minutes of one another in different parts of Kansas City. Now we'd be unable to just hop in the car and pop over to visit or help.

Allie's adoption was finalized on July 15, 2011. The next day we loaded two U-Hauls and headed to Atlanta.

I became a stay-at-home mom for the first time in my life. Grace was in first grade, and Reagan in second. The girls were resilient and loved the new adventure. Allie was the bundle of joy that allowed us to meet many new friends and neighbors. She was an easy and joyful baby, lighting up a room with her coos and smiles. We often got stopped by strangers who wanted to love on her. She had an energy about her that attracted others.

We settled into our new community, new school, and new life. I made sure to get back as often as possible to see family— and so Pam could see Allie.

All the joys and brightness of family were beautiful and sustaining presences, but for the first time in my life I was not earning my own money. This was both liberating and foreign to me.

I had supported myself to some degree since I was a teenager. Not working outside my home was hard. I felt like I had lost a big part of my life's purpose. I quickly fixed that by starting a clothing line for tall women. It was this new venture during my time in Atlanta that fueled my entrepreneurialism, opening a door for me to meet the gentleman who would have one of the greatest impacts on my career. Tom Hughes became my business mentor and a dear friend. He and his wife, Barbara, taught me more about business and philanthropy than anyone else. My stay there became a new time of growth and connection. We remained close until his passing, when he lost his battle with Parkinson's disease.

As much as we had fallen in love with Atlanta and Peachtree City, the community we lived in, the move was ultimately too hard. We had to travel to Kansas City every six weeks so Grace could see her dad, Tony; and Reagan, her mom. All the traveling exacted a toll on our schedules, especially since I had additional trips to make when Pam was available. It was all unsustainable. In 2012, we decided to move back to Kansas City. In 2013, Dale and I built a house there.

It was so good to be back closer to family and dear friends. Location did not slow down Allie in the slightest. As she started walking in her early toddler years, we noticed her strength, balance and athleticism all start to bloom. It became apparent that Allie had inherited Pam's God-given athletic talent. By eighteen months she was riding a two-wheeled scooter with the confidence and ease of a child over eight. She'd put on her helmet and go zooming down the sidewalk so fast that she gave the neighbors a fright. At two, she'd watch her older sisters play soccer—then, at home, drop kick a soccer ball in the backyard for hours until she perfected the movement.

Chapter 32:
Guardian

In 2013, on a particularly beautiful sunny day, I was at our home in Lee's Summit, a community about twenty minutes from Dad's place in Pleasant Hill. The family I'd been socializing with, who sometimes cared for the kids if I needed to run errands, were usually either under my roof or twenty minutes away in their home. Pam was sometimes nearby and sometimes not. Dale was traveling for work, while Reagan, Grace, and Allie were occupied in different parts of the house.

The phone rang and I answered it. No one spoke from the other end ... at first. Then I made out Dad's muffled voice. I had my car keys in my hand before he was able to convey what he needed—I knew something was very wrong.

In a series of short phrases, he let me know that Pam was there with him, and she was threatening his life.

With no one to take the kids, and time being of the essence, I gathered them up and we headed to his place. I parked a little way from Dad's house, around the side of the barn, so that the children wouldn't be too close. With the kids strapped in, grouped safely to remain in the parked car, and instructed to lock the doors, I raced up to the house.

I froze when I found Pam holding a knife and threatening Dad, who was calmly talking to her. I'd truly walked into a dangerous situation. *Have I called the police? Has Dad been able to?*

The same fire that raged in me back when Pam held a knife to my throat reignited at the sight of her threatening our father. Then, it hit me—I was not looking at Pam. This was the imposter, Addiction. I loved Pam; I hated Addiction.

Not an ounce of rational thinking remained for me. I reacted purely out of emotion. It carried me to what felt like one massive leap on top of Pam. The knife went flying through the air. Pam may have always been stronger than me—and the drugs that overtake the bodies of our loved ones often increase a person's strength—but, on this day, her strength could not hold a candle to mine. It felt supernatural. I was able to hold Pam down and keep her away from Dad until the police arrived—even though I wasn't even sure who had called them.

It was only after the police took over that I came back to earth. My thoughts returned to the children. Though they were safe in the car, the struggle was playing out between three officers and Pam. In front of them.

I was horrified to realize that the police cars and ambulance were in full view through the car's windows. Not only that: The fight she put up extended further onto the property, so the children clearly saw her being handled and then subdued.

She was escorted by ambulance to the hospital.

In that moment, I knew I could not do this anymore. I knew then that Pam would never be the same, and something had to be done for her safety and for the safety of others.

I called legal counsel and began the long application for guardianship. I would now take on the responsibility of having to make most—if not all—of her decisions, managing her finances, arranging her housing, getting her medical care, and trying to see to it that she did not have access to the drugs that had overwhelmed her life, or work hand-in-hand on all these issues with someone whose job handling them would be. Pam needed to be declared legally incompetent.

Shortly after that incident, Pam entered a lockdown facility where she had no other option than to get clean. It was a grueling six months for our family. To know that she was fighting this battle, and that we couldn't be in the ring with her, was gutting us. It was a sound decision that allowed us to breathe some relief into the rollercoaster roles we had all played.

Allie was two years old when the public guardianship for Pam became official. Pam was clean, but the drugs had already caused much damage to her mind and to her physical body. For the first time in fourteen years, we got a part of our Pamela back that we had missed: her sweet spirit, her kind heart.

The rage and anger she'd battled for fourteen years dissipated. It was so good to be able to speak to her on the phone. She'd ask how others were doing. She would talk about her day. Her speech was clear and coherent. She was interested and interesting. We loved sending her pictures Allie had colored, sending her photos, or sharing anecdotes about the children's activities. We could gift her things and know they wouldn't be sold. She started attending family functions again. Her re-engagement in her life meant she could also participate in Allie's.

I began to sleep well at night, knowing Pam was safe and drug free. I used some of my free time to learn more about drug addiction and the system. My advocating for Pam grew to take a larger role.

Part Four:
Storm Damage

Chapter 33:
Burnout

Overall, for me, it was great to be back in Kansas City. Though we mostly thrived as a family unit, I personally struggled with my self-perception and my roles in life. I would get involved in helping others, and then find myself tired and feeling frustrated. My body, mind, and soul were screaming at me to take care of myself first, but I did not know how to listen. Perhaps I didn't think I was worthy. My superpower was putting people back together again, or making it so people didn't suffer, or working out ways for them to not feel hurt by others. I was that one-person cheering squad for everyone ... except for me.

When I did take some time to slow down, I started questioning some of my own life decisions—especially those regarding the circumstances around marrying Tony and, later, Dale.

I deeply loved all the girls in my life, yet I found it difficult to know what to do in certain situations. When Reagan started processing her own emotions and was needing to understand her role in her birthmother's life—and in Dale's, and mine—I didn't know how to support her.

Dale and I married as best friends, and operated beautifully as a couple with a commitment to always support each other, but I still found myself in a personal state of wandering in the wilderness. Because I hadn't truly healed, I became my own worst enemy. I was seeking external validations for my internal struggles. Without my faith to anchor me, I defaulted to flight. When things got hard, I ran, not out of strategy, but out of survival. My wounds whispered lies louder than truth, allowing fear to lead my life. I wrestled with that, knowing that my life mission was to advocate for each of my children, as well as raise them. I took my responsibilities very seriously when it came to Pam's care.

In those months following Pam's institutionalization, the drought I was experiencing in my faith caused me to lose connection to God and the connection in his healing power and restoration.

But then, there was me. I had to address issues within my own self, in terms of my own self-care and worthiness. I'd been running on a version of empty for a long time—really running. No matter how beautiful and wonderful the children were, there were those separate parts of me that felt a void. I had to decide whether I could own them or not.

I began to realize that I sometimes had accepted what others would call *crumbs*. I had always believed that the reward for helping people was the part about helping people. I thought that being of service to others would take care of all the fallout—tiredness, irritability, sadness, worthlessness. I thought the joy from helping would fix all of those symptoms. All my life I'd dropped everything and run for everyone else's sake—I'd been a first responder of the heart-and-soul kind. I'd read about how emergency workers often experience burnout, but I hadn't quite recognized those signs in myself.

As I delved into this topic, I began to question the truths of my marriage of convenience to Dale. The way I chose to handle the results of my introspection was to turn away.

Dale and I parted as friends. We divorced in 2014.

The time had come for me to address some of my own demons. I started therapy. It was slow going at first. I accepted that I had been and was a work in progress—and I began entry-level processing.

I supported each of us getting help, including Grace. We had all lived a hectic life. There had been many loving people, but also inevitably a dose of confusion and frustration surrounding the multiple relationships within our blended and extended families.

In 2016, I purchased a house that became, so far, my favorite place I had lived since the farm in my early years. It was located in a dreamy neighborhood of Bent Tree Bluffs, with the best neighbors a single mom could ever ask for. Our home was nestled in a cul-de-sac of a family-friendly neighborhood full of kids and complete with the protection of retired couples who looked after us. Our next-door neighbor, George, became like family. A proud, full-blooded Greek, he opened his heart and his home to all us girls from the moment we met.

It started simply: We had a small dog, and that little dog always found ways to sneak through the fence. George would always help us chase after her. He started inviting us over every time he had a gathering at his house, which was often. We'd have dance-offs in his kitchen. He brought us into a world filled with friendship, laughter, and the kind of warmth that only a Greek spirit could bring. I felt like I was back on Malta; I felt like I was home.

George took us under his wing, teaching us about life, connection, and community. His driveway became a gathering place where stories were shared, laughter was loud, and friends became family. Every weekend, it transformed into a hub of activity, a lively space where neighbors, friends, and strangers were welcomed with open arms. His mother, Franny, became a third grandmother to my girls. Sadly, she would pass from breast cancer in 2024.

It was in this cozy Cape Cod–style home that I felt a sense of contentment and peace I had not felt in a long time.

Life began to calm for me, in the only way it can in a very busy person's life. We built solid and healthy routines. Dale remained a very steady presence in my life. He was gracious to me during this time of self-discovery. We were still friends despite the hurt I caused him. We co-parented so well that many suggested to us that we should write a book on co-parenting. Dale and I simply understood that co-parenting well was a selfless decision for the sake of the kids. We understood that the people who hurt the most when two people can't co-parent well are the kids.

Chapter 34:
An Unexpected Message

An unexpected email arrived one cold rainy day, while I was on a working lunch break at my new full-time job in finance. It was a short and sweet message, from a man, Greg, whom I had known for many years, but with whom I had not actually spoken in nearly a decade.

Would you like to meet for coffee?

I accepted the invitation.

Our many years of knowing each other had started when I was in high school. I was close to his family, and respected Greg for how hard he worked for his kids and how involved he was in their lives. He was very influential in our community. After college, I lost contact with him and his family, aside from occasionally bumping into them at a coffee shop or a grocery store, sometimes even a Friday night football game.

We met up for that coffee.

One coffee turned into two and then three and, before I knew it, this man whom I had admired and respected, began to capture my heart. The feelings of respect I had held for a man who I had seen, years ago, give abundantly to those in our community who were in need, who had balanced a busy life and career with coaching his children, began to shift toward love.

Unexpected love. A type that I had not experienced before.

I struggled with the new feelings for quite some time due to our age difference, and because of the platonic and mentoring relationship I had previously had with his family.

The emerging relationship was that of two mature adults with children. I knew in my own heart that this was healthy and permissible. But I was worried others would judge. I was concerned how the world around us would likely see only the differences, the should-nots.

As my feelings deepened, I feared the potential disapproval from family and community alike: a questioning of motives and intentions, and perhaps even suspicions about our past. This terrified me, as there had never been anything but professional and social respect between us in all the years I'd known his family. It took a good while, but those disapprovals finally grew much less real than the quiet understanding and connection we shared.

Loving him was about holding a connection that I knew was rare. Our caring was mutual and grounding. He had a steady presence, a wisdom I was drawn to, a way of listening that made me feel seen. It was as if he instinctively understood parts of me, without me needing to explain them. And yet, I still wrestled with the weight of others not understanding how a situation so unconventional could feel so natural to me.

I learned to accept that some of the joys in life come wrapped in complexity. That love involves courage. That love doesn't fit neatly into anyone's expectations. Once I accepted this, we decided to move forward with our relationship.

Two years later, in 2018, we married in an intimate ceremony on the island of Anegada, in the British Virgin Islands. A close group of friends and family attended.

Since that day, our marriage would be filled with great travel adventures, embracing new friends and family, new grandkids, highs and lows, good and not so good. The ups and downs of life and marriage would be spared neither for us nor for our relationship. We sadly would not last as husband and wife.

However, it was through these same trials that I relearned that the center of the peace in my life is my relationship with the Lord. It's neither the relationships we have, nor the amazing people we surround ourselves with, nor our careers, nor even our children. For me, it is my God and my purpose.

The people in my life bring me great happiness and joy. They fill my life with laughter and mirth, and sometimes with hurt and frustration; this is a part of being human and having relationships. For me, it is during difficult times in life where I grow. These have included relationship struggles; the worry that accompanies being a parent, concerns for a sister who is battling addiction, or merely the trials that are a part of everyday life in large, chaotic family systems.

It is through our struggles and the grace with which we navigate our path, that each of us can discover ourselves. I have learned to stop fighting challenges and difficulties and, instead, embrace them—always via a sacred and personal conversation with God, asking what He would have me learn in each season of my life.

Most recently, those conversations have allowed me to understand the role Greg has played in my life and to move, once again, to a place of peace within myself: a place where I can center myself as a mother, as a sister, and as a best friend to myself. There is a great deal of pain that comes with leaving a relationship and, conversely, a massive amount of courage which results in both finding and swallowing pride: the gaining of self-knowledge. I could choose to feel shameful about making a decision to leave my relationship, but I know that shame is neither healthy nor productive. Though I may have moments of self-judgment, I do not spend any time in regret. Decisions made for a healthy and authentic self move me forward. I am learning. We all are. I bear no ill will to anyone who has helped me learn on this journey.

Chapter 35:
Enough

In June 2023, Grace, Reagan, and I planned to spend a week in Greece for Grace's senior trip. Our bags were packed, but Grace's passport, sent for renewal eleven weeks prior, had still not arrived. After a solid three days on the phone trying to find any way imaginable to obtain her passport, we realized we were not going to have any success. It was time to pivot.

Twelve hours before we were scheduled to leave for Greece, I changed our plans and arranged for travel to an island that doesn't require a passport: St. John in the US Virgin Islands.

For the next six days, Grace, Reagan, and I lived in a wonderful villa. During our time at the pool, I noticed another family enjoying their time together. On the last day of our trip, I struck up a conversation with them after their sweet grandson threw a football my way.

The connection was instant—it felt like I'd known them my entire life. I learned that the mother, her three adult children—one son and two daughters—and their families traveled there annually to honor her late husband, who was the children's bonus father. After an entire day and evening of talking, I became privy to more of their story: how the mother and her three children had escaped an abusive first husband—the children's birthfather—when the kids were teenagers.

They shared their healing journey. I had never felt so moved and inspired by one family; it was obvious that their therapy journey had resulted in four emotionally intelligent and compassionate people. The proverbial life they breathed into me in just one day felt like enough to sustain me a lifetime. The son shared in more detail his journey with PTSD and how much he had overcome. His insight and wisdom were very therapeutic.

The overarching theme of that evening of conversation was *You are enough*. For the first time in my adult life, I began to finally believe I was enough. On the flight home, it became apparent to me that us ending up in St. John was no mistake. I was meant to meet them. Their vulnerability in sharing their healing journey sparked my own.

I got serious about therapy and contacted a highly sought-after therapist. Even though I had been seeing a counselor for almost two years, I knew a deeper dive was necessary.

Those subsequent two years of counseling with a male, Christian therapist laid the foundation for my true healing journey. He began teaching me the ways in which I have been a people pleaser: how I lacked boundaries, how I was not assertive, and how all of this, at times, contributed to a debilitating anxiety. I worked with him for a year and a half. Then, suddenly, his wife passed away. Her death turned his life upside down. He had to take a break from the practice to heal himself.

This transition led me to the most remarkable female therapist I could have ever known. She added to my therapy progress in a greater way than the previous therapist, and that's saying something, because he was amazing.

I began saying no. Setting much-needed boundaries. I became assertive, removing things that did not bring light into my life. The negative emotions of others began to have less impact on me. A new woman emerged as I reclaimed my life. I began to understand myself: my emotions, my own narcissistic path. My faith flourished as a result.

I went to people I'd hurt and attempted to mend relationships.

It grew apparent that when I loved and cared for myself first, my loving relationships with others also improved.

I purged drama, which reduced stress. In Marie Kondo style, I focused on minimalism in several areas of my life. Health, reading my Bible, exercise, and the word *no* became daily practices. This resulted in heightened respect from others, and for myself from myself. Meaningful relationships followed. Motherhood became intentional.

I finally told the Enemy, who had victoriously convinced me for nearly twenty years that I was fundamentally unworthy—and who had set up camp in my soul long before that—to go back to hell.

I diligently worked on me. My life changed so drastically that I could let this book finally emerge from my heart: a book I couldn't quite articulate back in 2020. What couldn't flow back then, poured out onto the page. Word by word, the truth unfolded and affirmed to me that my purpose was to inspire, encourage, and embolden others to come forward into their own truth.

I wrote about loving someone who struggled, of being in a family touched by addiction, and how that affected the dynamics of the whole. I worked on forming the story of my life and, as respectfully as possible, that of those around me—to share it so that others could understand the lasting effects of addiction, and the variations of healing. It felt as if God took the pen and guided my hand.

As I began to internalize being enough, the sun of life rose, and blessings appeared in every moment, right down to the hummingbird who visited me on my walks. Even winter—a season I previously found little beauty in—delivered joy. It was as though all my senses returned, holding a jeweled torch. My eyes opened wide. I began living.

Chapter 36:
Birthmother, Birthdaughter

Aunt Pam took great pride in Allie's budding athleticism. She beamed when we talked about Allie's gifts, knowing that Allie inherited them from her.

As Allie entered her preschool years, she liked playing with the boys because they tended to be more competitive, like her. She loved climbing, jumping, and running—it suited her to hang out with the guys.

When she was potty training, she had underwear with pink daisies on them. After months of refusal to use the potty, she asked for a pair of *Teenage Mutant Ninja Turtles* underwear. She put them on and never had another accident.

She continued preferring to wear boys' clothes. Her choices led me to create a clothing business for girls who wanted rough-tough clothing to fit their bodies.

Saying Allie was spirited was an understatement. At three, she knew what she wanted, how she wanted it, and did not think she needed to explain herself to anyone. She was the fiercest three-year-old I had ever met. I wanted to be sure that I helped mold her spirit, not break it—because there were times her developing spirit was a little too strong even for this spirited momma.

Allie dove into all things sports at three years old. She started playing basketball, soccer, and baseball. She played on a few coed teams, but ultimately wound up playing on all-boys' basketball and baseball teams. She was often the best on the team, playing better and running faster than the guys. She continued to play all-boys' until she was eight years old, and we started getting complaints from some of the parents because they didn't want her there. It was obvious that this strong little girl, in all her competitive glory, was making some of the boys unhappy because she was better than they were.

As part of co-parenting Allie, Dale and I attended her baseball games where she regularly hit homeruns and ran bases like Alex Gordon from the Kansas City Royals. At one of her games, a coach of a softball team approached us and asked if he could recruit Allie to his softball team. Dale and I discussed it and gave Allie the option to try out softball, which she vehemently declined. She said she wasn't about to play with a bunch of girls who cried when they got hit with a pitch. "I'm tougher than that," she said.

Through a combination of the coach's persistence and some of the parents' continued attempts at getting Allie removed from the boys' league, Allie agreed to guest play in a weekend tournament. She fell in love with the game.

From ages eight through thirteen, she played on an elite softball team and had the privilege of playing all over the country.

Later, the rigorous schedule and demands of softball caught up to Allie, causing burnout, and she decided to take a break from softball and explore two other sports she loved: basketball and soccer.

I imagine Allie's athleticism will be a shining light in the future. I won't be surprised if she uses her gifts on a large platform to influence and inspire others.

It's not often I see a lot of Pam in Allie's physical looks and appearances. However, occasionally, outside of her athleticism, I will catch a mannerism or an expression that mirrors Pam's. I enjoy seeing that certain way she smiles before she bursts out laughing, or her bright eyes light up even more, like Pam's used to, when she discovers something new. I enjoy having a front row seat to the slow reveal of Allie's purpose in this life. It is breathtaking.

⁊₭

"We talked about fear a little while ago," I remind her. "The fear of sharing a story. And we've talked about making meaningful message from the mess. I have been wondering: Were you ever scared out there? Everything you went through—that I know about—sure sounds scary."

"No, I wasn't scared of anything or anyone. I never was. Not before. And not during."

"I used to remind Mom and Dad of that when they worried about you, or when we hadn't heard from you for long periods of time. I used to say, 'It's PK we are talking about. She's tough. No one is going to mess with her; and if she needs anything, she will get it.'"

"Yeah, I was one of the toughest on the streets. I really wasn't scared of anything or anyone. It's probably why I am still alive. You have to be tough to live the life I've lived."

"You definitely were tough. And you still are."

"It wasn't all bad. I loved playing football for the Kansas City Glory. I was a badass. I think I could have gone on to play NFL. Probably coulda been the first woman to play in the NFL if I hadn't blown out my knee."

"You were and are definitely a badass. It kept me from worrying about you as much as if you'd been a wimp."

"I was never a wimp, Toots."

"Oh, I know!" I giggle. "I grew up with you."

"Those women I played against used to be scared of me. I didn't show them any mercy. I broke my ankle once in a game and kept playing."

"I didn't know that."

"Yeah, and dislocated a shoulder."

"You are a baddie. Allie always gets mad at me when I say *baddie.* She says, 'Mom, stop talking like you're a teenager. We don't live in the 1800s anymore.'"

Pam laughs. "How is Allie?"

She drifts suddenly to the window. *Time out. This is big for her.*

Now it's my turn to drift off. I have no idea how she is able to process the updates about Allie. She's happy for her. I know that. But I don't know the heartbreak inside.

"I asked, how's Allie?"

"Allie is great. She is amazing really; she takes after you, after all." We both giggle. "But not a day passes that I don't embarrass her. That's part of the teenage years. She's tough like you, though. She got her athleticism from you. She plays like you used to, and steals bases like you did, and hits a lot of out-of-the-park home runs. She's pretty special!"

"She does take after me, doesn't she?" *Is it pride I detect?*

"She sure does."

"I want to go to one of her games."

"We'll make that happen. Gotta get you a little stronger."

"I forget about all that," Pam says wistfully. "Don't know or remember all the illnesses I have. Does she know about my addiction and how I still struggle at times?"

"She knows you've struggled with drugs in the past and that you have battled with addiction over the years."

"Does she hate me?"

Pam has tuned out. I want her to hear the answer. Truly hear it. I don't want her falling asleep with that being the last phrase she spoke before she begins to dream. With that question lingering.

"Pam. Hear me now. How could anyone hate someone who gave them life? That girl is pure love. And so are you. Do not forget that."

I find a throw and pull it around her shoulders.

She doesn't have to ask me to leave. She needs some time.

Chapter 37:
Introspection

It was during my time in the wilderness that I made the most mistakes in life. My choices weren't anchored in my faith. Perhaps we're always in the wilderness regarding some areas of our lives. During my time in this wildnerness, I wandered far from the path God had intended for me. I took the long road: the one marked by dry seasons, heartache, and unnecessary pain. But even in my rebellion and resistance, He never left me. His love was patient, never forceful, but always present. I see now that while I may have delayed the journey, I didn't derail His plan. He still led me to the place He always intended, just with a few more scars and a deeper appreciation for His mercy. God's grace carried me, and He welcomed me back the moment I turned my heart toward Him.

In my twenties, in college, the shock of Pam's addiction faded into the background. There were still lots of unknowns, but as a family we had set boundaries with Pam—or thought we had.

Her psychiatrist told us that the various drugs had done such extensive damage to her brain that we could never expect her to be the old Pam. I let her issues go and settled into starting a family and raising my family and the stresses that came with my young adult life—for me that translated to college, my marriage to Tony, and growing my family.

However, Pam was always there in my thoughts. I believed I'd moved her situation to the back burners of my mind. Yes, I was busy juggling marriage, college, pregnancy; then parenthood and work—but though she disappeared for six months at a time and was often found living in different states, I'd always learn of it. Pam would touch base with my parents from time to time, even showing up to crash with them for a few days before disappearing again. Sometimes they would get updates from her through other family members that she would reach out to. Pam always kept in touch with our Aunt Sas, my mom's twin. Aunt Sas and Pam always had a deep bond and connection.

My parents took on a lot more of Pam's problems at that point. Dad once found out she was living in a drug house, retrieved her, brought her home, and then tried to get her help. It was always temporary: She spent my twenties in and out of rehab.

Some may judge us for not chasing after Pam, but you learn as someone who has a loved one battling addiction that at some point in their journey, you have to practice tough love and let them fight this battle on their own. We tried the best we could to fight it with her every step of the way, but there comes a point where you have to protect your own from the mental anguish they cause themselves.

This was taught to me by the most amazing and influential teacher Pam and I ever had in high school: Mr. Hickman. Mr. Hickman was the kind of teacher you never forgot. Revered by every student who walked through the doors of our high school, he had a rare gift for making each lesson feel like a conversation and comedy skit rather than a lecture. He was engaging, intentional, and knew how to make us laugh just as we needed it. His influence stretched far beyond the classroom: He saw potential in students before they saw it in themselves. He had a heart for Pam that mirrored that of our own father.

There was one defining moment for me with Mr. Hickman that would help me navigate my future with Pam. One day in my Junior year of high school, just before Mr. Hickman departed this earth from pancreatic cancer, he pulled me into his classroom to talk to me, after understanding all too well the path that Pam was heading down. He proceeded to tell me he had a daughter battling the same demons Pam was battling. He told me their story. The story of how he and Mrs. Hickman had a daughter who struggled with mental health and ended up battling addiction.

I didn't know it at the time, but the story he was telling me about his daugther would mirror the story that would become Pam's life. He told me about how her lifestyle began taking such a toll on him, Mrs. Hickman, and their other daughters that they had to learn to practice tough love. He taught me that a person can't sacrifice their entire life fighting the demons of their loved ones, that some demons can only be fought by the one they possess, and that you have to advocate for them and make sure they know that they are always welcome home.

Mr. Hickman taught me the greatest lesson on tough love that day. A lesson that I would lean on over and over again throughout the years.

We knew so little about Pam: if she had friends in this time, any serious lovers. Her changing tastes in favorite foods or movies or music; the details that connect us all, whether or not we are addicts or mentally stable. There was a period when she was an addict capable of these things—until suddenly she was no longer capable.

We'd talk about her addiction as a family, but did not let it consume us like it previously had—again, we'd tell ourselves we were not allowing it to. Yet, our hearts at the time were still holding pain—ours and hers—and our souls were still loving toward her and wanted for her to be well. We still had one foot in the past, wishing for miracles. Our faith had us believing we would be given that miracle. Seriously, as if she alone would overcome addiction when many others, equally valid in their beautiful humanity, could not. Perhaps that was where my advocacy seed was planted—to help one is to help all.

In Kansas City, as in many places across the nation, a person confined because of mental health issues could only be held for a certain length of time. This made it difficult to enter into any kind of consistent therapy—patients were discharged before any serious work can start.

Over the years, Pam has stayed in a hospital or medical facility in a segregated ward for short-term mental health patients, with the occasional longer stay of two weeks or thirty days. These stays are not long enough for her or for others who, in reality, require long-term plans.

But the system is even more broken now than ever. Mental health initiatives cannot seem to get new funding—and many existing programs have lost their funding, as have other parts of the medical system. People with mental health issues admitted to facilities might be dismissed in as little as a day or two. Many who need help are not even admitted.

When Pam wasn't receiving active treatment that included long-term goals and consistent programming, she always relapsed.

There were times when Pam brought dangerous people to Dad's home. One time, she invited a drug dealer to Dad's to get Dad to pay them because she owed so much money. It was terrifying for him and placed him in harm's way—plus they now knew where he lived. Because of episodes like these, I grew more and more angry with her. I was furious that she'd jeopardize our own parents' lives.

What I came to realize, as I got more involved as an advocate, is that many people view those with mental health issues as a lost cause. Beautiful humans who are addicted are dismissed because of their addiction. They become their addiction. The shift takes away the language based on humanity provided by patience and forgiveness, and becomes instead focused solely on treatment, or lack of.

I began to see also how family members trying to help their loved ones were not receiving nearly the amount of support they needed. I knew that I often felt undeserving of any help because I was not the one who was living on the street, sleeping behind dumpsters, not bathing for months, not eating well, or otherwise living in hell. It took time, but I came to realize that if I want to be a support to Pam, I have to accept help as well.

Like many others in my situation, I had sidelined or delayed my needs. I had not acknowledged my suffering or examined my own issues. I'd pushed away any fears of failure and of letting Pam down in some way I couldn't even define. I'd do this by busying myself with being as much as I could be and doing as much as I could do to make up for the lack of what Pam hadn't done or become. I doubled my contribution and didn't realize that was what I was doing until I almost burned out.

I had to realize that I didn't have to be ashamed for considering my needs.

Even as I started to put myself first, if I got into a jam, and wanted to complain—whether regarding a literal traffic jam or a disagreement with a family member—I'd still get that feeling that I should not complain because there were those worse off than me. *Pam* is the one suffering; all the counseling should be going to Pam.

Of course, this was not a healthy way to think. It was as though I'd chosen to live in a kind of martyrdom and pass that off as a life of service. I can only see that in hindsight. I was the girl and then young woman who had always tried to make everything right for everyone. The girl thrown into the role of family caretaker.

I'm not sure I would have let someone else help our family, even if they had come forward to do so—after all, helping was *my* job. I had been born with that servant's heart and I was the ultimate codependent. I believed that when I talked about any fears, emotions, or problems, I was just creating more drama, which then provoked more problems, so I did not talk about any of my own feelings of pain, disappointment, or perceived inadequacy. I was also fiercely jealous of my role.

I also worried about adding to the concerns of others. Even when I moved past my shame and embarrassment surrounding Pam's lifestyle—which had prevented me from talking about it—I began to unravel each time the subject was broached. It was difficult to simply ask, "Hey, has anyone heard from Pam?" in case it stirred something inside the person I was talking to, thereby causing them unintentional pain.

Chapter 38:
Maturity

"Have you ever wondered why Pam and not you?"

I've been asked this question so many times. My answer is always the same:

"No. I never have."

Even in my teens and twenties, I thought that her choices were hers. She was stealing from others and could be violent. I chalked that up to her selfishness. I couldn't see she was struggling. I only knew I wasn't going to make those choices.

I was certain that I was not Pam, and never would nor could be. But, if it is that easy to become addicted, if we don't know what brain chemical or genetic mix is triggered at a certain age to induce bipolar or other diseases, then what did I really know? Maybe I had hoped I was not next. The only thing I did decide for certain was that I didn't want to get into drugs. It's quite possible Pam felt that way too when she started using out of curiosity—she's hinted as much.

We played basketball, we had that in common. We would not both do drugs. We did not have that in common. I didn't think too much beyond that until my thirties when I began to develop more compassion and realized how arrogant my certainty was.

I was hypervigilant and suspicious of Pam when I was younger and her problems first surfaced. Yet later, in my late twenties, I became interested in the psychology of addiction itself—the questions we never asked when she first fell into its throes. I began doing my own research and reading anything I could about the addicted mind. I waited decades to question her on the cause of her condition, and then discovered there was no giant secret she'd kept from me. No anonymous attacker, no assault followed by threats. It had been curiosity, then the discovery of how it allowed her to feel in control. A life of perceived rather than real freedom. The shelving of all life milestones that had been open to her: career, professional sport, the world on a string. But the reality of addiction was not that blissful or easy for her, and I had never realized that.

⁂

How did I cope with what I learned happened to her after she became an addict? How can others deal with horrific news that creates indelible images inside the head of the family member—the one who learns of certain details?

The best way possible for me was through finding grace—with a strong side of deep breathing; I told myself and tell myself to go easy on the resentment. Embracing an understanding of life's journeys and its many turns.

Numbing with overwork, food, or substances is not a productive way to live, and it offers zero opportunity for growth. I found that acknowledging a trauma that occurred is a starting place. I then shift to being aware of my own feelings around that point and subject, addressing them before I dive headfirst into helper mode.

In the past, I have overworked and overperformed and over-delivered in all the areas of life I was involved with. They were ways to cope and numb the pain I felt for my loved one. Not all of that was productive, even though there were very positive results for other people.

What I was doing was postponing the reality required for self-examination, that could lead to accepting me as me, then truly growing into me.

I became a repetitive helper. Maybe I was addicted to helping. What I think is that I constantly recycled my responses to Pam's asking for things. Her manipulation for money, for being enabled. Manipulation was a way for her to survive—I get that now; it is still her go-to. She'd say she was getting her act back together and going back to school, turning her life around in some way. A laptop was required. Of course she'd then sell it. I wasn't helping her by allowing the manipulation. Yes, I wanted so hard to believe that this time it was real. No, I never thought she was a lost cause. I still don't. No one is a lost cause.

I always saw the pattern of manipulation, but it was hard to call her on it. After all, she was suffering, and I wasn't. After all, we'd had great times, and now I could have them and she couldn't. After all, we were family, and I loved her. These are the things we tell ourselves.

२६

When I was in my mid-twenties, Dad and his second wife divorced. Pam started staying more with Dad. Dad became Pam's rock during this time. He and Mom worked tirelessly to help her. I don't know how they did it. I think it is different for a parent than a sibling. I think my parents felt guilty, thinking they somehow contributed. We kept thinking if we helped her enough, she'd come out of it. We thought love would win, but the reality is, Addiction operates in a completely different arena than Love. Love always wins, but Addiction writes the rules of the game.

I know with certainty that I will never stop loving Pam or fighting for her.

❧

"Are you sure she doesn't hate me?"

"No, PK. Absolutely not. She could never hate you."

"I hate myself for it."

"Please don't hate yourself. Any one of us can get swept into addiction. Nobody chooses that life, PK. Allie admires you for choosing life for her. She is grateful to you for asking me to adopt her. She doesn't look at you in a bad light at all." I glance at Pam, who is staring at the floor. "When we talk about you, we typically talk about the fun stories of our childhood. She loves those. I tell her about how you were so good at sports that people watched you even if they didn't have kids or grand-kids playing. I tell her about how, when I watch her play, she reminds me so much of you. Her mannerisms, her determina-tion, her playing style. She always smiles—and it is genuine.

"I tell her about all the times we played basketball for hours late into the night. I tell her about how we walked to town when we lived in the country because we wanted candy from the grocery store. I tell her how we used to go crawdad hunting all the time and bring a bucket full of them home. I tell her that story about you attempting to perform brain surgery on the cow. She always laughs and asks me to tell her more and more stories. She loves you, PK. She will always love you."

"Really? You think she really loves me?"

"Yes, PK. She doesn't tell you as much now, because she's a teenager. Teenagers can be distant at times, and fussy, and seem uninterested." I lean over and touch her arm. "Listen, PK, if I had a penny for every time she told me I was being annoying or embarrassing her, I'd own a small island. She's coming out of that teenage funk and starting to really blossom and get super funny and more witty. Like Dad. She's fun to be around. You'll start seeing her more interested again in talking with you on the phone or wanting to hang out more when you come for visits. As parents raising teens, we often question if they love us." I snort. "Welcome to the teen years. You remember those years with Mom. She used to annoy us so much." I draw out the *so much* for dramatic effect. Pam doesn't laugh, though.

"Yeah, she did a lot for me too, just like Dad."

"She did."

"She was always so patient with me, especially when I was living with her. I was awful. I used to take my druggie friends over to her house a lot and we acted stupid or smoked weed in her house and ate all her food and terrorized her a little bit. I feel bad now, thinking back. But she was always patient with me. She got upset, but I knew I could always go home if I needed to. That's one thing I never had to worry about. I always knew that no matter how mean I got or how much trouble I caused everyone, Mom and Dad always welcomed me home with open arms. You all never gave up on me. I had a lot of friends over the years whose family disowned them or made them feel awful and stupid, but you guys never did that to me. I have the best family, and I don't know what I'd do without you."

"We are family. Remember that was the song we always danced to at family weddings? 'We Are Family.'" I sing the title. "That part about having all my sisters. That's one of many things I love about our family. We were one big, loud, loving family. We fussed and fought at times, but loved hard, and never disowned. Maybe boundaries and tough love at times, but never disowning."

"Yeah, without family, I'd be homeless and probably dead."

I let her words hang in the air for a moment before I speak. "We've always done everything to keep you from that. Here we sit, and I have asked you to recall your stories. Now you understand why? Talk about love, and the present has more meaning. I'm so grateful for it."

"You're my angel. You saved me and you gave Allie a beautiful life. A life I could have never given her—and I love you so much for that. You're so smart and beautiful and you have done so much for me."

I try to swallow away the lump forming in my throat. "I mean, thank you. I'm your sister. And you've done a lot for me too, PK. For all of us. You've helped us see the suffering in the world so that we can work to help others. You gave us Allie. We wouldn't have Allie if it wasn't for you. Look at all the blessings God has given us through Allie's life."

"Yeah, I did bring Allie into this world, didn't I? She did get her athleticism from me, didn't she?" *There's that repetition again.*

"She sure did."

"I used to be scared that she'd find out all the things I've done—and there are a lot of things I've done that I don't want her or you to know about. But I want to help people too. Just like you have helped many people. I want to help people who are on drugs or who have sisters or daughters on drugs too. I want to help people through your book."

"Our book."

"Our book?"

"Yes, our book. I'm proud of you for being so brave to want to tell more of your story. You're a strong woman. I know you've been through a lot, but we all have messes in our lives. We all do things we wish we could take back, or hurt people in ways we never intended. God wanted me to do this for years. I'm thankful you chose to be a part of it and are brave enough to tell your story. "You're my hero, PK. I tell Heath he is my hero for serving our country. I'm telling you that you are also my hero. You're my hero for choosing life for Allie. You're my hero for being so brave and strong to ask me to adopt Allie. Even in the midst of the pain and struggling, I can see so clearly that God has still used every part of your life for a purpose, just as He always does."

Chapter 39:
In the Wilderness

Until recently, I didn't have the clarity to put together a review of my own life-map. I think entering your forties is an invitation to reflect.

After my divorce from Tony in my mid-twenties, I was wandering the wilderness. Just as the Israelites had wandered the wilderness for forty years after being freed from slavery in Egypt, I too wandered the wilderness of my faith.

As a Christian woman who had believed deeply in the institution and sanctity of marriage, the reality of me divorcing my first husband left me shattered—it deeply fractured my faith and personal identity. Our teaching of marriage as a sacred, life-long covenant turned it into a foundation of security; when that foundation cracked, so did my belief system.

I wrestled with feelings of shame, failure, and guilt. I believed I had fallen short of God's ultimate design. There were people in the church who also were quick to judge; feeding my sense of shame. It was as though I was suddenly greeted with betrayal from many people in my life. I am grateful that my time inside it did not last forty years; however, it did last a long time. What I discovered from wandering for more than eight years is that God had never left me, even though I abandoned Him. Instead,

He revealed Himself to me and taught me to trust in Him—and to trust in myself through Him.

Restoring my faith ushered in the restoration of who I truly was in the present moment, and set the tone for the future me. Through the process of piecing my life together, I found a new understanding of my faith and resilience. I learned that a life apart form God is what the enemy wanted. The enemy wants us to feel shame, failure, and guilt. The enemy wants us apart from God.

The shattering of an ideology allows for a rebuilding that acknowledges the depth of grace, healing, and unconditional love that God offers, even amid our brokenness—hence the kintsugi. God's love was never tied to the perfection of my marriage or ideals that were out of my control. God's love poured gold into my cracks, creating a more valuable me. I became a journey: a human journey of faith, rediscovering my worth and identity in Christ alone, not in marriage or through a particular life plan.

That season of struggle brought an opportunity to rely more deeply on God's strength and less on my own. To embrace a new path where I found, even after tremendous heartache, that God's love and plans for me remain steadfast and true. This did not mean there wouldn't be more struggles—we are human beings, doing human things, and we create contrast and conflict in this life.

Following my restoration of faith, therapy helped me understand the aforementioned importance of boundary-setting and assertiveness: key components in discovering who I wanted to be.

Restoration meant restoring my core: a core which included my values that contained my faith, and which were contained by it. To restore something is to re-story something. We are re-storied through our pain.

Pam received a new story called *Allie*. Allie gave Pam a new story called *Purpose*. I'm convinced Pam would not be alive today if it was not for Allie.

Pam was part of my own restoration. She trusted me to raise Allie. She gifted me her own heart by asking me to become Allie's mom.

The negative events that happened in my life had purpose. Difficult times were perfect catalysts to push me into purpose and further shape who I would become. My pain shook me up and lifted me, then set me down in a better spot. A less angry one. A less judgmental one. A more fulfilling space with a wondrous view of life. I learned I have more strength than I thought I had. Knowing I would always have more pain ahead of me, I hoped I might recognize it as a continual driving force for the maintenance and renovation of me.

One of my favorite verses is John 16:33. It describes the night before Jesus goes to the cross, as he is talking to his disciples. *I have told you these things, that in me you may have peace. In the world you have oppression; but cheer up! I have overcome the world.*

God accompanies me everywhere I go. It is the greatest part of my identity. Yet I could say, too, that I go everywhere with community, with heart, with soul, with hope. I had strayed away from those things—and those became my wilderness years. I came back and through, bringing that wild beauty of pain with me.

I kept returning home to a knowingness—a solid belief that challenging situations help us learn what we need to learn. I believe in free will—therefore I knew God neither gave Pam her addiction, nor handed her a punishment. In one way, she chose it. Just as in other ways, she did not.

In my first book, *Nova: The Courage to Rise*, two teenagers gaze upwards into the star-filled night, seeking comfort and answers. I realize now that none of us hold all the secrets of the universe; even as we are most definitely a part of those secrets.

⁊⁊

I seem to reflect better when I'm high above the world. That bird's-eye view of life allows for a perspective I don't get when my feet are on the ground. The same friendly flight attendant is leaning over.

"You are a writer, then?" She's making the rounds to check if seats are upright and trays locked in place.

I tuck away my notebook and smile.

"Hope it's a bestseller," she says.

I smile at her, but the truth is, I honestly wish it never had to be written. That all the heartache and everything related to addiction did not exist. I aim and toss a couple of rolled-up sheets of paper into the trash bag she's holding.

"What genre is it?" she asks.

I am caught by surprise. I wasn't expecting any questions. I guess I'll have to get used to that. Let's see, I'm aware there's an arc … I have been determined to not make my premise preachy. I'm aware that there is an arc in every book that mirrors the hero's journey. Overall, I've realized as I write, that I have to ask myself, "Who is the hero of this story?" That is its premise. *The reader*, I finally decide, after much thought.

She dips down and in, perhaps to give me or my answer privacy.

"It's a love story," I say.

Chapter 40:
Return to the Dog Park

Yesterday I was in the air. Today, I'm on solid ground

Dog parks are amazing spaces that hold so much joy. Dachs-hunds and Dobermans, street rescues and show-worthy Samo-yeds are unclipped from their collars and set free to sniff anything and everything, chase frisbees, and generally cut loose. These loyal pets get to chat it up with their own kind. The dog park is such a joyful place that all the dogs' humans can relax too.

Like the time I met the gentleman who asked me about Allie, and ended up sharing his concerns about his own daughter's mental health.

I like to think I'll meet other people there from whom I can learn and who can learn from me.

⁂

I launch the ball from its cupped thrower.

"Look at them go," says the gentleman. "Our dogs are having so much fun."

"They're getting used to seeing one another here," I say.

"I've brought treats this time," he says. "I hope these are okay." He takes out a plastic bag of kibble-y things.

"Wow, thanks. Mine will gobble them up!" I take a swig from my water bottle.

"No daughter this afternoon?" he asks.

"She's hanging with friends. A teenager now," I respond.

"She's okay, though?" His grandpa-like concern is touching.

"She's great, actually," I reply. "Can I ask how your daughter is doing?"

"I'm glad you asked," he says. "I've had some time to think about what you said about your sister. Talked to my wife about it. We've decided we don't have to feel shame or be afraid to speak about her. Goodness knows, we have enough to be concerned about."

"That makes me so happy," I say.

"I still remember the day she was born. Such a miracle. I cried. Tears of joy. And I wondered if I'd be a good enough dad."

"Oh, I know what you mean. I was there for Allie's birth."

"That's so wonderful," he says. "I made a promise to her that day that I'd always take care of her, be there for her. Recently, I've made another promise that, no matter how much she's been through, whatever the issues, no matter how much she thinks her life has fallen apart, I won't let her carry that as shame for the rest of her life."

"That's so good to hear. Shame is often what truly holds us back in life."

"Forward," he says. "We're moving forward, though it might not look that way to other folks."

"Everybody's healing story and recovery is individual," I say. "You know, every memory I have of my early childhood includes Pam. We were truly inseparable. We shared a bedroom, clothes, passions, and dreams. I was convinced that I'd never live a day without Pam by my side. I was even considering a career as a surgeon's assistant if that's what it took—she was going to be a surgeon. I was never without Pam. Until I suddenly was. Then I had to figure out how to find her again, and through that, I had to find myself."

"Just look at those silly dogs," he points out ours chasing one another around. "Living in the moment."

"You gotta love that, hey?" I am close to tears.

"No judgment. No grudges." As he smiles, his eyes follow the dogs' impulsive paths around one another. "My wife and I have signed up to go to a meeting that's coming up—a presentation at the main library. It's about housing for those with mental health issues. Thought we might like to get involved. Know anything about it?"

"I happen to know a few things about it," I say. "I hoped I'd run into you because I was going to put that possibility out there, and invite you. I've been working on a few things in that area. Well, more than a few. I've had some meetings with the mayor and other civic administrators. There's a pilot project I want to establish that will see an unoccupied building transformed into a housing and health center. It's in its early stages, but if this plan is successful, it could prove itself a template for many more. Not just here, but across the state. Maybe even inspire nationwide action."

"Well, you can count on us to be there," he says. He calls in his dog, who instantly races to his feet. He bends down to his mutt's head and buries his face in the animal's long fur. I look away. I give him time to release his emotions—relief.

I tear up. I'm no longer in the wilderness. I've been praying for clean for so long—and now I'm making things happen for healing. This really *is* a love story. A never-ending one. There will be more joy, and there will be upheavals. Both on the same day, even.

Part Five:
Advocacy in Action

Chapter 41:
Meeting Each Other
Where We Are

ASAM—the American Society of Addiction Medicine—defines addiction as "a treatable, chronic medical disease involving complex interactions among brain circuits, genetics, the environment, and an individual's life experiences. People with addiction use substances or engage in behaviors that become compulsive and often continue despite harmful consequences."

Our loved ones appear as data points in pie charts and graphs of national health treatment centers and feature in sociologic and scientific studies all over the world. Those statistics can be helpful: There is strength in numbers; great sadness too. While the data reflect the number of people affected, they do not nearly begin to illustrate the number of stops and starts, cries for help, almost-deads; nor the level of investment, broken hearts, severed ties, and unconditional love that come with the territory of addiction.

Like many other concerned family members all over the world, I seek to understand my addicted loved one to the best of my ability.

My personal journey has shaped me as a sister and driven me to become my sister's advocate, ensuring her voice is heard in the systems that often overlook or fail people like her. The direct work I did guided me to a larger role: to advocate for all people caught in a broken system.

I refuse to believe our system cannot be repaired, rebuilt, or reinvented. I know that brokenness can be fixed, even if the cracks show—especially if and when and where they do. I know creativity can invoke genius and innovation. Developers—from software engineers to architects—do it every day.

The overhaul required for large systems that are supposed to serve our marginalized is not a quick fix—I get that. Yet, small innovations will ripple-effect and change the world. The work that is ahead of me will have a local effect, but then can inform larger regions. There is no reason why it cannot reach all the way around the globe.

I've spoken to doctors, psychiatrists, guardian ad litems, counselors, social workers, case workers, and mental health professionals. When I explain that I'm trying to understand the system better so I can advocate, most laugh an awkward *say something to fill the silence* laugh, then, in a patronizing voice, wish me good luck.

Acceptance of a broken system makes for tired people and dead-end roads. The mindset of apathy and acceptance of brokenness stokes the fire in me. I refuse to accept a laugh and good luck as an answer. I intend to ignite creatives, to inform everyone from doctors to designers, and issue a wakeup call. I intend to gather and promote innovative ideas.

According to the United Nations Office on Drugs and Crime's *World Drug Report 2024*, one in eighteen people in the world had used drugs in 2022, and one in eighty-one people had a drug use disorder—an increase of 3 percent from 2018. At the same time, only one in eleven people with drug use disorders received treatment for it. People who battle mental health issues and addiction deserve better. The families who fight tirelessly to help their loved ones deserve better. Society deserves better.

If we all endeavor to understand how systemic brokenness impacts those who are struggling—and by extension, society as a whole—we would start to see real and lasting change. Why have we, as a society, allowed our friends and family and strangers who have these battles to be left behind? In many ways, we have abandoned those who need us most. Those who can't fight this battle alone. It's disgraceful—and I refuse to accept it.

Thinking as a whole: That's the key. We are part of that whole. Until mental health struggles and/or addiction affects a loved one, people pursue other interests. A group mentality quicky labels those unhoused, or bouncing from street to rehab, as *lost*.

Newsflash: We are, or were, all loved ones.

My sister's plight could be your spouse's after they have surgery and find it difficult to stop using prescribed pain medication. One decision your child makes at a party after they've just clinched MVP in their championship sport can change their brain chemistry—you might not recognize their personality by their next birthday, summer vacation, or next Christmas.

We are all in this together.

※

Once Pam became violent with our dad, it became clear that her battle with mental health and addiction had reached a point where she could no longer make effective and healthy decisions for her own well-being. After multiple periods of homelessness and countless attempts to help her, we realized that, without intervention, she'd remain on the streets, lost in a cycle that was not only dangerous, but also unsustainable.

Her security is still a challenge in our lives.

I began the arduous process of working with my parents and the state to make Pam a ward of the state of Missouri. Pursuing guardianship for my sister was one of the most challenging and emotional choices I've ever had to tackle. I felt this was too difficult a decision for my parents to make, so I took the reins. While it was an arduous path to walk, filled with bureaucratic hurdles and heartache, it was a necessary step to ensure her safety and access to the care she desperately needed. Through this process, she was removed from the dangerous environments that fed her addiction, and for the first time, she was placed in a residential home with access to mental health services.

This guardianship allowed the system to step in and help her to clean various drugs from her system and start on a path of recovery. It wasn't easy, but it was lifesaving. She's lived in a few places, and will likely reside in more. Through this intervention, Pam was given a second chance at life: a chance to live with dignity, receive ongoing mental health treatment, and experience a better quality of life. It allowed us peace of mind in knowing that the chances of losing her forever to addiction were significantly reduced.

That was only half the battle—and not without the inherent emotional dilemma related to respecting her adult right to certain freedoms.

Funding shortages and lack of imagination have affected communication between hospitals, group homes, and lockdown facilities, and have severed many necessary links between medical care, psychological counseling, and individual planning for each person to live with dignity.

Money talks. But funding is not the only thing that is needed. Staffing requires money, but well-created programs that are innovative and measured for efficacy are needed for any money to show a return on investment.

While I'm grateful that the US government has or had some systems in place—Pam might not still be here otherwise—our working systems need to receive attention and funding to stay in operation. Those who run the systems must be asked for input to recreate, restore, renovate, and innovate the programs. A coalition of frontline workers, along with representatives from all areas of life—from addict to architect, from banker to builder—must come together to listen, and only then, co-create.

※

During my ongoing efforts to advocate for improved mental health facilities, I started collaborating with the Governor of Missouri and the Mayor of Kansas City on a new initiative. Together, we intended to identify and acquire a series of empty buildings that would be transformed into dedicated mental health facilities. These facilities would serve as vital resources for attending to those in need, addressing the severe shortage of mental health housing in our state.

What would make this initiative unique was the involvement of private donors who shared our vision. I was working with individuals and organizations to provide the funds needed to refurbish these spaces into fully functioning, state-of-the-art mental health facilities. Once completed, we would begin working with the state of Missouri to manage them, ensuring they remained sustainable and accessible to those who needed them most.

This kind of partnership between local and state government, private donors, and community advocates like me demonstrates a new way forward in addressing the mental health housing crisis. It's about pooling resources and creating lasting, tangible solutions for our community. By working together, we can provide much-needed support for individuals and families facing the challenges of recovery from mental health issues and addiction.

A functional platform for those with mental health issues and addiction didn't exist when Pam began battling the disease. I am grateful that work on building a framework has been started.

My parents, brother, and I were left without much direction or education on these topics. Although so much has changed for the betterment of mental health and addiction issues, we need to continue to raise awareness and reduce stigma.

Advocacy begins with education—including simply listening and learning from those who are experienced within a subject.

Stigma reduction is crucial for encouraging people to seek the help they need without fear of judgment and shame. Any amount of effort creates a positive ripple effect.

People suffering from mental illness and addiction face judgment due to widespread misconceptions. By promoting understanding via discussions with friends and family, social media efforts, community outreach, and volunteering, we can change perceptions and foster change.

Diligently promoting policy changes—including the offering of solutions—and better funding are issues that mental health organizations deal with all the time. It must seem to them like an uphill battle in which representatives with great ideas keep getting knocked down. I am proud of each one of them who stands up and keeps going.

Expanding healthcare coverage for mental health treatments, increased funding for mental health services, and better mental health housing solutions need to be prioritized. Supporting organizations who partner with lawmakers is paramount to implementing systemic change. Any amount of support, large or small, makes a difference. Many believe they don't have the time or resources to make a change, but tiny interjections of effort—like a fan-out for a lost child—can begin to rebuild what worked and reinvent what didn't.

We owe our fellow humans—our loved ones—three meals a day, a place to sleep, and access to undoing or managing conditions they never wanted or asked for. We owe them dignity.

My next step in advocacy is to begin working with established organizations on the promotion of mental health education in schools. Early intervention is critical. If only one student out of an auditorium recognizes and is impacted by a presentation, then that is one more loved one saved, and another ripple out there influencing other students.

By combining a multitude of advocacy strategies, we can create more compassionate communities and systems, and then subsequently provide the care and support our populations dealing with addictions and mental health need to thrive. Advocacy work is the foundation of substantial, lasting change.

Chapter 42:
A Meth Crash

Addiction is like selling your soul to the devil. It shackles everything pure and good about a human and unleashes the dark side
that comprises every possible class of selfishness.

In the throes of an addictive episode, it is as though the
person you knew and loved no longer exists and is consumed by
darkness. In the case of long-term addiction, it is devastating to
witness your loved one's physical body and mind suffer various
effects over time: five years, ten, twelve, twenty-five.

ð

I see you and hear you.

Let me hold part of that pain by acknowledging your pain.

ð

In our case, it has been horrific to watch Pam's physical health
decline so rapidly for her age. And it's horrible for Pam to see
the pain we are in, knowing it comes from witnessing hers.

I also see my parents eaten up with guilt, thinking there is
something they could have done differently to keep Pam from

this destructive path. For family members who are not directly involved in her care, they are still marginally involved simply because they know and may not know how to address it. This can look like avoidance. They almost never mention or acknowledge the elephant in the room, with the exception of Aunt Sas. Aunt Sas talks to Pam every day. She nurtures Pam. Pam often spends the night with Aunt Sas when she comes home to visit family. I really do admire the bond that lies between Pam and Aunt Sas. The love shared between them is magical and it is unconditional.

Watching stress consume nearly every part of the life of a parent of an addict is torture. For my family, it has sometimes felt like we climbed onto a rollercoaster over a quarter of a century ago, and though it slows, we can't get off; we just got used to it over time.

I've spoken to many addicts who explain that even after an addiction is overcome, it is a lifelong battle to remain clean because that monster never fully releases its grip. One recovering addict told me, "You have to fight like hell to dig your way out of the hell addiction placed you in, and you slide back in many times before finding a way out—if you ever do. And even after finding a way out of addiction, it finds a way to accompany a person the rest of their life. Sometimes through shame, sometimes through relapse, sometimes through physical ailments. It leaves a trail of destruction as if a storm blew through. Even when a former addict thinks they've cleaned up, life is never the same."

A trail of destruction as if a storm blew through. That is a visual for me. We live in the Tornado Belt. I picture the storm building and passing through the geography of the self. A phenomenon that goes beyond the strongest wind, the wettest rain, and the darkest days.

If we can clean up after storms, and study them through the science of meteorology, surely we can also perform clean up within the self. We can begin to expand studies on addiction to include community connections, and involve the family members who are struggling to help their addicted loved ones. The healing thread here is in the togetherness of effort. Trying to overcome addiction alone is pretty much unachievable—maybe there are exceptions, but life and peace exist on the other side of emptiness, longing, and lack of fulfillment.

ᖚ

Recently, Pam had some issues related to methamphetamine use. I learned what a meth crash is after Pam spent three solid days in bed without even getting up to eat. We were convinced she was dying. After the fourth day, one of the residents in her home explained to us what Pam was going through.

The meth crash can be as dangerous as using meth itself. Put simply, a meth crash is the severe psychological and physical—mind and body—exhaustion that follows days or weeks of heavy methamphetamine use.

First, the meth speeds up speech and thought, sending the addict into a rapid-breathing state where they feel all body processes rushed. As the drug wears off, the speeding-up slows down and halts, almost reversing its effects, precipitating a complex series of symptoms. The first few days of the crash are the worst as the body tries to return to some kind of normal or homeostasis. The crash can begin within 24 hours after using meth—that's how fast the withdrawal starts, that's how needy the body and mind are for the meth, how addictive it can be.

Even after the crash, the brain chemistry remains altered, and a person can struggle with functions like memory and mental health issues like depression.

꙳

When Pam and I refer to *meth*, we're talking about methamphetamine, not methadone—yet both are opioids. Not everyone has a general understanding of opioids. It's on the news, but those are short pieces that don't have explainers to differentiate.

Sometimes people might go to meetings and hear certain terms, and then be afraid or embarrassed to ask what they think are basic questions. Don't hesitate to ask questions when you go to meetings. Everyone deserves to have clear information. We helpers do not have to be scientists to understand the basics of what we hear.

Likewise, when information is passed by or through a group of people—someone tells someone tells someone—the information can get skewed. Even searches on the internet may not include correct citations or contain 100 percent factual information. For that reason, expert resources have been used to share information of those basics. Nothing daunting, but informational enough to explain the terms the professionals in your loved one's life might use when they talk to you.

Chapter 43:
Moving Again

December 26, 2024. This is a day when daydreaming really helps.

"I don't think my new coworker likes me, because I'm assertive and set boundaries," Pam says as we head to the dock to watch the sunset.

"A lot of people don't like assertiveness or boundaries, but boundaries are healthy," I reply.

"I hope she comes around. If she doesn't, well, that's her problem, not mine. I don't adjust my boundaries for the comfort of others," Pam says.

"Listen to you! You sound like my therapist, and that's a huge compliment. Try setting boundaries and being assertive in your forties, when you haven't practiced either your entire life. It really upsets people. It only took me four decades to figure that out," I say.

"You've been learning a lot in therapy, huh? You know I may seem on top of things, but I see a counselor too," she explains.

"For the stress you have as a surgeon, that's quite under-standable," I say.

"No, Toots. For some pressures I had when I was a kid. And for some concerns I have about my mental health—depression," Pam gently corrects me.

"You've not mentioned this before," I say.

"I'm mentioning it now," she says. "Therapy is preventative as well as healing. But there's still a stigma around it. Especially for those who work in a hospital setting. You'd think they'd be the first employer to get serious about health and prevention of illness."

"Thanks for keeping me up to date," I tell her. "I'm here if you want to talk about it more."

"I know," says Pam. "Here for each other. Always have been. I wonder what it would have been like if one of us had, you know, slipped. There was a lot of pressure on both of us. Me with the athletics and school, and you ..."

"What about me?" I ask.

"To have to follow in those footsteps. As Pam's sister. To not be yourself," she says thoughtfully.

"I was my own person. Mostly. I loved your coattails. And the free tickets." I laugh at the memories of our perfect lives that were often chaotic.

"I'm chairing a meeting on funding for the unhoused, those with mental health issues. My new friend, Brian, has a daughter who has some serious problems. Will you come?" Pam asks.

"If you want me to. If it's important. I mean I've got a gazillion other things going on with the business," I say.

"It's an epidemic," says Pam. "Someone has to do something. I'm telling you, any of us could end up there."

"Not us," I say.

"Us." She stops walking. "Look, we've both got children. I've got Allie. You know I was a little wild when I became pregnant, but I could have been wilder. What if I had been and couldn't keep her? Tricia, it could have been me. Now, it could be Allie. It could be your girls. Wake up, Tricia. Smell the coffee, or in this case, the meth. I'm gonna send you a video."

"You sound serious. Let's walk some more. I promise I'll come. Is it that easy for anyone to, well ... slip?" I ask.

"You'll see. I'll send you a documentary. You'll see how it could have been you. Or me," says Pam. "Now, about this sunset."

We round the corner. We both grow quiet. I pull the blanket from my backpack and spread it on a slope of grass near the water. We lie on it, side by side, just like when we were children. Silent, both taking in the sun and its reflections. Magnificent in every sense.

"It looks like God graffitied the evening sky. Look at all those colors," Pam whispers.

"He's the ultimate artist. The edge of that cloud looks like a rose petal," I say.

"Let's stay until the stars come out," Pam says.

"Then you can tell me a story." I squeeze her hand, and she squeezes back.

Oh, God in heaven, what I'd give for that scene. I'd trade every sunset I have enjoyed for this to be true. Even if it meant I were blissfully ignorant of the issues I've come to advocate for. But it is not true for us. Neither is it true for many others. This is why we have to talk about mental health struggles and drug addiction. We must tell our stories and, as Ram Dass says, *walk each other home.*

Thank goodness for daydreaming, fantasies, and gratitude. Thank goodness for prayer and action plans.

Yesterday we celebrated Christmas Day 2024, and this morning—the 26th—before forty people showed up at my home for dinner, Dad and I had to move Pam to another home.

A few weeks ago, the day before Thanksgiving, her guardian emailed me to let me know Pam was being kicked out of the home due to poor behavior. I didn't want to read the rest, but knew I had to.

She'd compromised the security of the nursing home. That's the polite way of saying it. Other residents were feeling uncomfortable, and the staff were concerned too. Pam was confrontational. What a kind way of saying she was yelling and fighting.

That's also the euphemistic way of saying all the things that were in print for me to read.

Friends who did drugs in her room.

Dealers showing up to collect money.

Breaking curfew and waking others to let her in.

Her guardian explained that he knew she was being evicted, but was not being proactive to move her, because Pam had a way of pulling on his heart strings. He had a compassion and empathy for Pam that sometimes clouded his ability to make the difficult decisions for her. I didn't condemn him for it; I was grateful she had a guardian who cared so much for her.

I phoned him and said I would do my best to handle it. Then I made some more calls and found a room at an assisted living facility that offers less freedom and more rules. One where staff will ensure she takes her medications. She knows this place; she was there before, during the pandemic. The place houses primarily those who are mentally ill and those battling addiction. The residents are more in her age range. She has no friends where she is at; maybe she can make or find some there. She has been so lonely, fueling her desire for the drugs that provide relief to that loneliness.

When we get there, the place indeed has 120 residents, many who are close to Pam's age. She immediately recognizes a few she'd made friends with when she lived there before.

A not small part of me feels guilty, having known that a nursing home with eleven other residents much older than Pam was not the right place for her. Pam's guardian ad litem worked tirelessly to ensure she had a roof over her head. The problem is, Pam was blended into a community of seniors. Their needs are different. It was not fair to either them or her.

It took almost three weeks for her paperwork to be transferred and everything to be finalized.

Mom and Dad share caregiving duties while I have the phone attached to my ear to make sure all the i's are dotted and the t's are crossed.

Mom and Dad are likely exhausted. I know I am.

As the dishes soak in the sink downstairs, and I drop into bed, I think about how this is another upheaval—one during a holiday period, when I am in celebration mode and busy as can be. Oh, Pam. Sweet, dear Pam.

 ⚘

Her situation remains precarious. Her body, once full of fight, now moves slower—worn thin by the relentless weight of addiction. The years have left their marks: invisible scars etched deep within her, organs already in failure by the war she never stopped waging. I can see her strength dimming, not for lack of will, but because her body is tired. It's as if her physical self is waving a white flag, even while her spirit still clings to the hope of one more good day.

When I get over myself and my busy-ness, I am reminded of the meaning of the season and how poignant the timing: the last chapter of the book; the posada. Mary and Joseph's search for a place to stay mirrors a little of Pam's housing crisis. My thoughts take me to considering all those who do not have a place to stay—not even a stable. I want to cry—but mostly I want to love. That is what I choose to do. And will continue to.

Part Six:
Resources

Basic Terminology

It is difficult to sit in a doctor's office—they do not often have much time to go into explanations—or attend a meeting, such as Narcotics Anonymous, when you are confused or uncertain about the meanings of words that get tossed about.

Pam and I believe this is a valuable rabbit hole to travel down because not enough people feel comfortable raising their hand or interrupting a doctor to ask: *What is an opioid? Are the poppies in my garden dangerous? When someone says* meth, *does that mean methadone or does it mean methamphetamine? What is the difference?*

Opioids are a class of drugs including both legally prescribed and illegal ones. Opioids include heroin, oxycodone (Oxycontin), hydrocodone (Vicodin), codeine, morphine, fentanyl, methadone, and methamphetamine.

These drugs, by binding to receptors in the brain, are powerful painkillers that can create strong feelings of doom and provoke intense elation. They are highly addictive regardless of whether they are obtained illegally or via a prescription.

This brings us to **poppies**. And we know people wonder but can be shy to ask about them. Opioids come from or are created to mimic the natural substances found in a type of poppy plant called an *opium poppy*. Not all poppies are opium poppies. The opium poppy, *Papaver somniferum*, is a large annual—meaning it has to be planted or seeded each year. It produces a narcotic sap that is used for illegal drugs. The perennial poppies that come up every year in your garden are oriental poppies. Another poppy, the California poppy, *Eschscholzia californica*, is from the same family as the opium poppy but does not contain opioid compounds. There are capsules, tablets, teas, and an extract that people produce from this plant which are promoted as helping with pain and with sleeping issues, but which lack large studies to prove their effectiveness or long-term safety.

Many associate the opium poppy as the raw material for opioids, and that's true. Those raw materials are combined with other chemicals in regulated scientific labs to create semi-synthetic or human-made opioids, including hydromorphone, hydrocodone, and oxycodone. Illegal chemists also use labs to produce heroin, which is derived from altered legal and regulated morphine. Then there are illicit labs—think basements and garden sheds all the way to high-tech, under-the-radar, illegal operations—in which chemical products are remixed and cut into other chemicals to put dangerous product on the street.

Opiates are therefore the class of drugs derived from the naturally occurring opium poppy plant that creates the active ingredient in the drugs. Common opiates include opium, heroin, morphine and codeine.

An opioid drug is a substance that can be derived from the poppy plant, be synthetic, or be semi-synthetic, meaning the active ingredients are created chemically in a lab. Common opioids include morphine, oxycodone, Oxycontin®, hydrocodone, and fentanyl.

All opiates are opioids, but not all opioids are opiates. But opioids and opiates have the same effects on your body because they have similar molecules and they both have high addiction potential.

Fentanyl is a synthetic opioid—meaning it's artificially manufactured to mimic what is in the opium poppy—and is fifty to one hundred times more powerful than morphine. In clinical settings, fentanyl is used for treating severe pain—as an end-of-life sedative and for end-stage cancer.

As a street drug, the many deaths associated with fentanyl are related to its strength and the inability to distinguish its presence when mixed with other drugs.

Methadone is a synthetic substitute given by prescription for pain and widely used to treat opioid addiction. Methadone programs may be suggested for your loved one who is addicted. Under supervision, the controlled administration of methadone can help someone reduce their opioid dependency. Though methadone is still an illicit drug, it is the supervision and dosage that allows a programmed amount to be reduced, over time, until the addict is no longer dependent on it. It works by bonding to the same brain receptor areas that other, stronger opioids do and thus blocking a craving.

Amphetamines were first sold over the counter in the 1930s to treat nasal congestion. Later they were developed and used to treat what we now know as ADHD—attention deficit hyperactivity disorder—because of their interaction with the central nervous system. They function by stimulating the components of the nervous system to produce increasing amounts of dopamine, norepinephrine, and serotonin. These qualities make them drugs with massive potential for misuse.

Methamphetamine is made from amphetamine. This is what is meant when people say *meth.*

Illegal methamphetamine is produced to create an exaggerated response from the body—a powerful sense of euphoria. It is manufactured so that greater amounts of the drug get to the brain, resulting in harmful effects to the nervous system. As a street drug, it is also often mixed with a variety of other components, making for even more dangerous situations. Its combination with fentanyl has proven fatal for populations worldwide.

It's produced in a variety of forms, from pills to powder and crystal forms—like crystal meth. Easily made in home labs, users quickly become addicted and develop a tolerance—which means that they need a steady supply to remain in a version of *addicted stable*. Without the supply, a drug user can quickly go into withdrawal, or what is called a meth crash, as we saw in Pam's story.

NOTE: Fentanyl test strips (FTS) are a solution that can help prevent drug overdoses. They are small strips of paper that a person can use to test if the drug they are using has been mixed with fentanyl.

The same type of test strip is also available for **Xylazine**, which is a non-opioid sedative used for animals. It is another drug mixed with cocaine, heroin, meth, and even with fentanyl to increase the street drug profit, and to make the high even more potent, addictive, and dangerous.

The Signs

Whether there are support systems in place or not, it's imperative that we all be familiar with the signs of mental health issues, whether they are related to addiction or not. It's paramount for grandparents, siblings, friends, and parents to understand, and then act on, changes in our loved ones—with hope that they would do the same for us.

Some physical signs of addiction in youth and adults include:

- Frequent illness.
- Fatigue.
- Slurred speech.
- Runny nose or nosebleeds.
- Sores or spots around the mouth.
- Sudden weight loss.
- Skin bruises.
- Excessive and constant sweating.
- Vomiting.
- Seizures.

Meth mouth is a term for when users have mouth sores and even gum disease and tooth decay.

Short- and long-term side effects of opioid addiction include:

- Drowsiness or sedation.
- Dizziness.

- Nausea and vomiting.
- Constipation.
- Physical dependence. This often manifests with withdrawal symptoms when opioids are discontinued or decreased.
- Tolerance. As you take repeated doses of opioids, you require increased medication to experience the same effect of pain relief.
- Respiratory depression. This can occur in healthy people, especially with higher doses. However, people with COPD, asthma or other lung conditions may be even more susceptible to fatal respiratory impairment.

Uncommon side effects of opioids include:

- Hyperalgesia, which is an increased sensitivity to feeling pain and extreme response to pain. Chronic use of opioids can lead to this.
- Delayed gastric emptying, which is the process by which the contents of your stomach are moved into your small intestine.
- Muscle rigidity.
- Immune system and hormonal dysfunction.
- Myoclonus, which are quick, involuntary muscle jerks.
- Arrhythmia.
- Pruritus, or itchy skin.
- Xerostomia, or dry mouth.

Long-term effects can include:

- Chronic constipation.
- Sleep-disordered breathing (SDB).
- Increased risk of bone fractures.

- Hypothalamic-pituitary-adrenal dysregulation.
- Increased risk of overdose.

❧

The behavioral signs of substance use are also visible, but they don't have a direct influence on the individual's health.

Most of the behavioral signs affect a person's social life, including relationships with friends and family.

Indicators include:

- Sudden difficulties in communication and interactions with family and friends.
- Loss of interest in school or work.
- Avoidance of eye contact when, in the past, the person was fully engaged.
- Poor balance.
- Insomnia.
- Cutting ties with others.
- A person may neglect their appearance when previously their hygiene practices were stellar, and/or they had expressed themselves via dressing as a fun and outgoing individual.
- Requests for money, without an explanation of what it's for, or missing money—even theft.

It can be difficult to tell the difference between teenage angst and drug use, but there is often a sudden noticeable change attributed to the situation rather than a gradual teenage change that involves challenging the adults in their lives.

There are situations in which a person who has had surgery and been on painkillers can become addicted to their medication. This will show with a slow recovery and even a lack of enthusiasm to get back into life. Previous users who have relapsed can often lose interest in family activities, their career, and their hobbies.

Sudden money problems can indicate that disposable income and savings are being used for drugs—and reduced or negligent financial accountability.

Blood pressure changes, mood swings, rambling, or rapid speech can also indicate a change.

Aggression can also be telling, either an escalation of aggressive traits or an out-of-the-blue personality change in a previously passive person.

꒰

Were there signs of these issues or symptoms in Pam's life? At first, those signs overlapped with what adults around us described as teenage angst, rebellion, Pam's strong personality. Her anger was seen as a feistiness that was rooted in her competitive nature; her poor marks as a sign that maybe she was overloaded and under pressure, so she needed a break. Her challenging authority and lack of respect were harder to explain, as was her change in hygiene. I don't think anyone close to her, at first, thought she was using drugs—just that she was breaking away with a new group of friends. When her schoolwork lapsed and her healthy habits deteriorated, it worried those of us close to her, but not to a great degree. When the severity of the issue became clear, her feet were firmly planted in the soil of Team Escape—she was already addicted.

Even then, I think a lot of people in her life who knew her as an incredible performance athlete, thought that she'd beat it. They wrote it off as a phase, because she was so talented and an expert in balancing her life; she was exemplary when she studied, practiced, and communicated. They did not realize she was sliding, or they thought the slide was a short detour.

This is the complicated thing about addiction: There are all kinds of paths of entry; no one is to blame for not seeing when it begins.

What To Do
If You Think It's Too Late

I have been heartbroken for Pam a thousand times. I've imagined how awful for her not to go to college, not to reach her goals of becoming a surgeon. I've wondered when she knew it had disappeared for her.

A life together as sisters, raising our children together, coaching our kids in sports, calling each other every day to have girl talk, became less and less likely. Everything slip sliding away. I didn't want to accept that. I had to find a way to reframe our relationship.

I've learned that the first casualty an addicted person suffers is often the loss of connection to the positive people in their lives. They may regularly lie and even steal from those closest to them. They begin burning bridges and isolating themselves. Pam was no exception. She spent years associating mostly with the people who helped her score her next high, while she withdrew from the people who were her biggest supporters.

It's hard to write about the years that robbed Pam of a fruitful life—a life of purpose. It's hard to write about the pain and anguish our family experienced during those years.

When Pam started her journey of addiction, if there existed a platform for talking about mental health issues, our family didn't know about it. It was true then—and is now—that many families find their situation embarrassing and are ashamed to share the way addiction affected them. I know I was.

There was a stigma around mental health issues. Decades after Pam's decline started, there still is. So much so-called care in the US has been shame-based, punishment-based. We know a lot more now than we did before, thanks to new technologies for brain scans, compassion-based clinical research, advances in genetics, and so on.

For example, we know that risk-taking behavior itself can be associated with at least a dozen different genes in the body, most notably the DRD4 variant 7 gene, associated with both heroin addiction and thrill-seeking behavior such as paragliding, risky sex, or cave diving. Early childhood experiences can alter brain chemistry, even differing in siblings who share two parents. We know that concepts such as body dysphoria, shame around sexuality, social isolation, and other factors are highly associated with first or continued drug use. So can diagnosable conditions such as bipolar disorder.

Learning about these predispositions can help alleviate stigmas when discussing a loved one's drug use with other people inside and outside of the family or social circle.

۳

It's never too late for love or forgiveness—even if a loved one is already near the end of life, or has passed. Some people find that advocacy for all works to help them move forward by providing dignity for others with mental health struggles. That advocacy can transform the lost voice of your loved one.

Others may not have the emotional energy to full-on push ideas or seek funding, but they can still support those who do.

There are ways for the supporters of loved ones to heal them-selves:

- Small donations—clothing, toiletries, cash to supporting agencies—or a small sponsorship at a fundraiser.
- Volunteering on a helpline.
- Talking to others to spread awareness and listening to others to increase knowledge.
- Writing a letter to a loved one—even a letter that loved one may never read—is therapeutic. As the saying goes: The pen is mightier than the sword.
- Seeking counseling for the self—and following through with it—is hugely important; connecting a voice to your heart is therapeutic.
- Taking stock of the parts of your own life that are not related to or connected or defined by the loved one, is invaluable.
- Mindfulness and meditation are avenues for overall peace of mind.
- Exercise is a great way to strengthen the system and maintain your own mental health.
- You can even write a book.

Most of all, I suggest you find every possible way to head down the road of Forgiveness and take a right at Gratitude. Open your heart and eyes and ears to seeing and listening. Use periods of silence as intentional times for your own observation of the unhoused, the addicted. Read all the loved one's messages. Attach personal learning to their needs.

Forgive as far down the disgusting drug-manufacturing chain and cartel that you can. Forgive the human condition, the brain. That energy generates the love needed for advocacy, no matter how small you might think the supportive action.

And if you can, try to never discount the power of prayer, whatever from that takes for you: I have experienced a tremendous amount of profound insights and healing through my faith.

Speaking Up
for Those Who Cannot

There is a precarious balance when we speak for someone else. Not as an interruption, but as an advocate.

Proverbs 31:8-9:

Open your mouth for the mute, in the cause of all who are left desolate. Open your mouth, judge righteously, and serve justice to the poor and needy.

One of the reasons I shared so much about Pam's and my childhood is because it exemplifies a strong foundation. A strong foundation is crucial for enduring life's inevitable challenges. Our strong foundation has become a resilient support system. What we have cannot crumble because of the beauty of our connection. Therefore, as her advocate, I bring both our hearts to the table, or microphone, or page.

I must examine the conditions and situations in the context of each individual situation and life experience when I advocate for others. It's important for me to remember that not everyone had an idyllic farm, a basketball hoop, or grandparents whose homes were community centers for their large families. And I have also to remember not to idealize that. There were tough times, including the loss of family members and divorces.

There is also this: The mental health system is one topic, and Pam's life is quite another. Every individual who is challenged with addiction and/or mental health issues is unique, with their own story. One thing is for sure: They are not the system. They are beautiful humans whose participation in the world is valid and whose lives deserve to be valued.

One of the first strengths any advocate needs is learning to be proactive and realistic. It's essential not to approach an issue from a victim mentality—no one wants to create new policy with a blamer or an excuse-maker. Positivity and well-researched facts can augment human stories.

Understanding the addictive personality is a must for those who want to advocate for those who are addicted. That way, the necessary holistic approach can be utilized when analyzing what is needed for services, housing, and various levels of recovery.

For example, despite twenty-five years of addiction, Pam is remarkable; she's lovable and people are drawn to her. She can also be manipulative when she's directly under the influence. These are key things to consider when finding housing for her: She wants to socialize, but she can also use those friendships to a negative advantage.

Her recovery, like that of others, has its own identity.

Recovery is not one straight or bumpy line for anyone. One hundred clients of a future recovery center will define, plot, redefine, and replot their journeys ahead. Recovery does not mean *clean from now on or nothing*. Clean or bust: That's a pretty hard target for a helping organization and system that is intended to be inclusive.

Given the criteria that recovery is a fluid process, then recovery and healing are possible even for people who relapse. This is a difficult stance for hard-liners to take, many of whom do not believe that drug addicts deserve housing or care unless they are clean, with no failure.

When I discuss this with Pam, though her diagnoses indicate that her own future is medically tenuous, she says, "Recovery and healing are possible. I plead with those who are dabbling in drug use, or who are battling addiction, to understand that it is possible to find healing and overcome addiction—but that trying to do it alone is impossible. I believe in life and peace on the other side of the emptiness."

These words are from the philosophical Pam who has been to hell and back, and who has been open to letting others in. She gives credit to those she has hurt—including me—and to those who have found forgiveness and hope through their relationships.

I advocate because I see what Pam has gone through. I know that others have gone through variations of that horror. That she can speak about recovery as she does is itself a testament to hope.

Pam is not a lost cause.

Your loved ones are not lost causes.

They deserve a collective voice to come together with the movers and shakers within government and private agencies who want to see a reduction in addiction statistics—and fewer people on the street.

Organizers, funders, and advocates need to understand that those in recovery will regress.

Advocacy is a powerful word and a huge responsibility. Advocacy involves actively working to support, represent, and improve the lives of individuals affected by these challenges. It means raising awareness, reducing stigma, influencing public policy, and ensuring access to resources and support systems that empower individuals to seek help and find healing. For families, advocacy means pushing for support networks and resources that help them understand and support their loved ones. For individuals, it may mean speaking up to share vulnerable personal experiences and championing reform.

Where to Find Help

There are various organizations and programs that work with addiction issues in one form or another. Countries usually have programs that do this on the national level, and often also at the regional or local level.

In the United States, I found the following to be invaluable resources:

Research

National Institute on Alcohol Abuse and Alcoholism (NIAAA): As part of the National Institutes of Health (NIH), the NIAAA is a federally funded organization that conducts or funds the majority of US-based research on the causes, treatment, and prevention of alcoholism and related issues.

National Institute on Drug Abuse (NIDA): The NIDA funds drug abuse and addiction research. As part of the NIH, this organization is federally funded and is focused on providing sound, scientifically proven advice to those living with addiction.

National Association of State Alcohol and Drug Agency Directors (NASADAD): This private, not-for-profit organization supports the development of alcohol and drug abuse prevention and treatment programs across the United States.

Institute of Behavioral Research: This organization operates as part of Texas Christian University. It evaluates the effectiveness of drug and addiction treatment programs and administers an array of studies within its community.

Office of National Drug Control Policy (ONDCP): The ONDCP falls under the Executive Office of the President of the United States, and oversees policies and objectives for drug control and prevention programs throughout the United States.

Research Institute on Addictions (RIA): As part of the University of Buffalo, the RIA studies alcohol and substance abuse issues with a focus on their relationship to family dysfunction and violence.

Substance Abuse and Mental Health Services Administration (SAMHSA): This federal agency—a branch of the Department of Health and Human Services—works with each state to provide resources to those living with substance and behavioral addictions. It also assesses community risk factors and intervenes when necessary.

Treatment Research Institute: This nonprofit organization focuses on conducting research and developing new methods to treat addictions. It also works to reduce the negative effects that addiction has on families and other relationships.

Addiction Treatment Helplines

SAMHSA National Helpline: A free and confidential helpline that's available 24 hours a day to provide referrals to treatment options and other important resources.

Veterans Crisis Line: Urgent help from qualified responders for military veterans and service members, as well as their families and caregivers, facing substance abuse problems or other mental health crises.

988 Lifeline: This 24-hour helpline offers prevention tools and live support for those in distress.

Crisis Text Line: This text line offers referrals and advice for individuals facing crises, including drug- and alcohol-related issues.

Partnership to End Addiction: Provides text, email, and phone support for parents and caregivers of teens and adolescents facing addiction issues.

National Drug Helpline: This helpline offers live 24/7 support for individuals seeking help with the recovery process.

Addiction Recovery Support Groups

Alcoholics Anonymous: The AA can connect you with local meeting centers or online support groups.

Narcotics Anonymous: Narcotics Anonymous can help you find a local NA meeting and provide recommendations for other resources in urgent situations.

Self-Care

It is ironic that self-care comes last—in this book, as in life. Sad, too.

I have been overinvested in the happiness of others.

I am a person who regularly wears rose-colored glasses and is working on being a reformed people pleaser. In hindsight, I can acknowledge the sense of frantic neurosis I accidentally created in trying to protect others from feeling hurt around family matters involving divorce, loss of life, or Pam's struggles. This took a toll on me as much as on those around me. It pulled me away from my own essence. Many times, regarding being kind to myself, I've either forgotten, not bothered, or have simply been too tired.

Every time I was or felt compelled to hold space for the whole world, there was nowhere for me to stand. Eventually, I had to fall: It was inevitable.

There were points in my life where I had no idea how to care for myself. I took the spiritual gift of a servant's heart to an unhealthy level. My reference of a servant's heart doesn't refer to someone who is lesser or demeaned; it reflects the posture of someone who willingly chooses humility, compassion, and self-lessness in service to others, just as Christ did. I kept busy from the moment I woke until I dropped to sleep—and sometimes I didn't even sleep. This led to a state of self-neglect, in the name of helping.

The challenges faced when helping loved ones navigate treacherous territory include ensuring there is a level of self-protection. It has become important to me to know when to step back, whom to reach out to when there seems nowhere to turn, and how to slow down and recharge.

I have shifted my energy, over time, to balance myself and my own needs and my compassion. When I'm dealing with someone who is experiencing their own unique hell, I now step back and assess what I need for myself before I jump in without thinking. It has taken me time to develop self-care skills, including getting professional help, so that I can remain in a good headspace while helping others. There is great pain involved when we witness our loved ones hurting—and we can feel that pain vicariously as caregivers. I have learned that, no matter how painful, it's hard for me to help someone without burning out unless I remember to care for myself first. The latter is still very difficult for me.

Information overload is exhausting and overwhelming. I've made the mistake of assuming I know how Pam or my parents feel. I have learned the terms, I have memorized the drug types and their effects, and looked into treatment types and recovery options. Yet I will and can never truly know how Pam takes in the information I provide her with in my helping.

Even regarding Pam sharing her story, I must caution myself to separate my knowledge and feelings from what she says. I cannot discount her truth of the experience, moment by moment.

Each of us who is an advocate, official or unofficial, can fall into the trap of thinking we know what is right for our loved one. That we can know what will protect them or is best for them—such as a secure facility with 24/7 care preventing them from accessing drugs, therefore making them clean, or rather forcing them clean. However, even if we have our own addiction story, we cannot ever know what getting clean under our own power and outside interventions and institutional supervision is like. Every person is different, every institution is different, every director is different, and so on.

Those of us helping our loved one do so while walking a fine line of decision-making, because it is foreign to us to grasp that our loved one may wish to remain in a squat, on the street, or drifting.

Scientists know a lot about the brain, but not everything—and not nearly enough yet to cure addiction or eliminate mental illness. On a personal level, each of us may have quite a bit of information about our loved one, but at the soul level, we have to admit that their inner thoughts and emotions are not ours. Ultimately, with all the best intentions I've had, there were plenty of times when I thought I knew what was best for others when I didn't even know what was best for me.

What is in my healthy power and serves me to be a productive helper is walking the aforementioned path of self-care before I attempt to step in and help. Only then can I truly have the energy to love to the best of my ability. I can strive for radical acceptance of others, and I can love unconditionally—which for me means being compassionate and knowing that tough love is part of unconditional love. I can create boundaries and take responsibility for them. I can increase my knowledge in all areas that interest me. I can recognize when I am overwhelmed: shortness of breath, irritability, sleep disturbances. I can even daydream to help me seed my future actions.

Awareness of where I'm at on this journey we call life. Self-love and acceptance of my limitations are keys to my thriving. They fill my pockets with the gold that God melts to fill my cracks—instead of creating spaces that absorb light, the light can reflect. That is what I strove for in telling Pam's story for her.

Bibliography

"Addiction." Cleveland Clinic, March 16, 2023. https:// my.clevelandclinic.org/health/diseases/6407-addiction

American Society of Addiction Medicine. "Definition of Addiction." American Society of Addiction Medicine, Inc. 2019. https://www.asam.org/quality-care/definition-of-addiction

"Amphetamines." Cleveland Clinic, March 24, 2025. https:// my.clevelandclinic.org/health/drugs/23039-amphetamines

Lusher, J., C. Chandler and D. Ball. "Dopamine D4 receptor gene (DRD4) is associated with Novelty Seeking (NS) and substance abuse: the saga continues..." *Mol Psychiatry* 6, 497–499 (2001). https://doi.org/10.1038/sj.mp.4000918

Mayo Clinic. "Drug addiction (substance use disorder)." Mayo Foundation for Medical Education and Research (MFMER), October 4, 2022. https://www.mayoclinic. org/diseases-conditions/drug-addiction/symptoms-causes/ syc-20365112

"Methadone." Substance Abuse and Mental Health Services Administration, March 29, 2024. https://www.samhsa.gov/ substance-use/treatment/options/methadone

Mosel, Stacy. "Is Drug Addiction Genetic?" American Addiction Centers, April 1, 2025. https://americanaddictioncenters.org/rehab-guide/addiction-genetic

National Institute on Drug Abuse. "Fentanyl DrugFacts." National Institutes of Health, June 2021. https://nida.nih.gov/publications/drugfacts/fentanyl

National Institute on Drug Abuse. "Methamphetamine." National Institutes on Health, November 2024. https://nida.nih.gov/research-topics/methamphetamine

National Institute on Drug Abuse. "Opioids." National Institutes of Health, November 2024. https://nida.nih.gov/research-topics/opioids

National Institute on Drug Abuse. "Xylazine." National Institutes on Health, September 2024. https://nida.nih.gov/research-topics/xylazine

"Opioids." Cleveland Clinic, May 27, 2022. https://my.clevelandclinic.org/health/drugs/21127-opioids

"The Signs of Addiction." Hazelden Betty Ford Foundation, 2025. https://www.hazeldenbettyford.org/addiction/signs-and-symptoms

United Nations Office on Drugs and Crime. *World Drug Report 2024.* (Vienna: UNODC Research, 2024), https://www.unodc.org/unodc/en/data-and-analysis/world-drug-report-2024.html

Acknowledgements

Unexpected Gift

If I could rewind and
freeze in time your joyful and spirited soul
I would place it in a bottle and never let it go
I would capture every memory we shared and
string it around my home
just to be reminded of all the laughter
and land we once did roam
I would carefully open the bottle
to show Allie a glimpse inside your soul
that has been hidden and masked for so many years
by the drugs that played a role
but only for a moment
would I leave your soul exposed
out of fear the serpent would slither in
shackling your soul foreclosed
Just like a thief in the night
addiction took you away
our hearts completely shattered
our minds fraught with dismay
months would pass without a sign
of knowing if you were okay

on our knees we would plead for the
Lord to bring you back someday
years went by with never a sign
of seeing the slightest shift
until one day
our prayers were answered
with an unexpected gift
the Lord took your brokenness
His grace shown through the cracks
by using the birth of Allie
like gold
binding your wounds leaving no gaps
the ultimate kintsugi artist
He highlighted the scars of your past
to reveal all the ways only He
can heal a brokenness so vast
even though addiction is still your captor
we know without a doubt
that someday you will receive a new body
then with praises we will shout
Holy is the Lord Almighty
she is free at last
and into the lake of fire
the pain and suffering will He cast

— Tricia

About the Author

Tricia Jacobson is an award-winning author, passionate advocate, and voice for those navigating life's hardest battles. Her first book, *Nova: The Courage to Rise*, won the International Impact Book Awards 2021 for Young Adult and Female Empowerment, inspiring young women to find their inner strength in the face of adversity. It was also third-place winner in the Firebird Book Awards 2021 in the Coming of Age and Young Adult Fiction categories.

Beyond her writing, Tricia has spent over two decades advocating for vulnerable populations. As the founder of 816 Loved, a nonprofit dedicated to empowering disadvantaged teen girls, she works to instill confidence, resilience, and self-worth in the next generation. She's also co-host of *The Matriarchs' Podcast*, a fun, inspiring podcast for teen girls and young women, offering real talk, life lessons, and empowering advice.

Tricia's commitment to advocacy extends deeply into the world of mental health and addiction recovery, where she champions improved housing, better treatment options, and policy reform to support individuals battling addiction, as well as their families. She collaborates with local leaders to repurpose vacant properties into mental health facilities, ensuring long-term, sustainable care.

A proud mother to four daughters and a grandmother, Tricia understands the profound importance of faith, resilience, and unconditional love. She lives in Kansas City, where she continues to write, speak, and advocate with the firm belief that even in our brokenness, beauty and hope can rise.

You Might Also Enjoy ...

ingeniumbooks.com/NovaRise

Beth Granger

"... captivating and heartbreaking."
— Sarah Edmondson,
Scarred: The True Story of How I Escaped NXIVM, the Cult That Bound My Life

BORN
AND
RAZED

Surviving the Cult was Only Half the Battle

ingeniumbooks.com/BORN

"UNFORGETTABLE PROSE, MASTERFULLY COMPOSED."
CORA TAYLOR, AWARD-WINNING AUTHOR OF *JULIE* AND *SUMMER OF THE MAD MONK*

LITERARY TITAN
BOOK AWARD

MARIE BESWICK ARTHUR

LISTEN FOR WATER

ingeniumbooks.com/lfwp

Jack F. Rocco M.D.

RECYCLED

A Reluctant Search for True Self Through Nurture, Nature, and Free Will

ingeniumbooks.com/recycledbook

THE **PROMISE** OF **PSYCHEDELICS**

DR. PETER SILVERSTONE

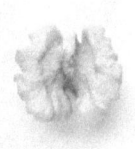

Science-Based Hope
for Better Mental Health

ingeniumbooks.com/0ugf

Come Passion

The Soulful ART *of* Healing Trauma

"...a must read for any clinician interested in a brief, effective treatment of psychological trauma."
Kevin E. Kip, PhD, VP Clinical Analytics, University of Pittsburgh Medical Center

Colleen E. Clark
MSW, RCSW

ingeniumbooks.com/cpaz

"An uplifting page turner!"
Heidi Hackler, author *Food, Mood, Gratitude*

A Memoir of
Survival and the
Kindness of Strangers

12 ELEPHANTS AND A DRAGON

Dr. Vi Tu Banh
with Marie Beswick Arthur

ingeniumbooks.com/12ED

LAUREN S. CLUCAS

CH♥ICES

HOW TO MEND OR END
A BROKEN RELATIONSHIP

"POIGNANT, POWERFUL, PRACTICAL!"
Verity Price, author *Present with Power*

ingeniumbooks.com/CHCS